WIT, *Whimsy* & WISDOM

A WORD*Girls* Collective

Wit, Whimsy & Wisdom
©2021 by Kathy Carlton Willis
www.kathycarltonwillis.com

ISBN-13: 978-1-7330728-3-0

Published by 3G Books, Beaumont, TX 77706
www.threegbooks.com

Scripture quotations marked NLT are taken from the Holy Bible, New
Living Translation, copyright © 1996, 2004, 2015 by Tyndale House
Foundation. Used by permission of Tyndale House Publishers, Inc.,
Carol Stream, Illinois 60188. All rights reserved.

Scripture quotations marked ESV are from The Holy Bible, English
Standard Version. ESV® Text Edition: 2016. Copyright © 2001 by
Crossway Bibles, a publishing ministry of Good News Publishers.

Scripture quotations marked MSG are taken from *THE MESSAGE*,
copyright © 1993, 2002, 2018 by Eugene H. Peterson. Used by
permission of NavPress. All rights reserved. Represented by Tyndale
House Publishers, Inc.

Scriptures marked NKJV are taken from the New King James Version®.
Copyright © 1982 by Thomas Nelson. Used by permission. All rights
reserved.

Scripture quotations taken from the Amplified® Bible (AMPC),
Copyright © 1954, 1958, 1962, 1964, 1965, 1987 by The Lockman
Foundation. Used by permission. www.Lockman.org

Copyedited by Kathy Carlton Willis

Editing, Interior, and Cover Design by Michelle Rayburn
www.missionandmedia.com

A WORD*Girls* Collective

Foreword by WordGirls Founder, Kathy Carlton Willis

WIT, *Whimsy* & WISDOM

A 12-Week Devotional to Shine the Light on God's Word

3G BOOKS

Contents

Worship & Prayer

Humor

Family

Spiritual Growth

Women's Issues

A Foreword by Our Founder

Devotional books are like artwork—finding beauty there is subjective. We hope our quiet time with God will be transformational. What contributes to a *God-wow* moment for one reader might seem mundane to the next. Our desire is for you to find nuggets within these pages that make you think, inspire you to worship, and even give you a few laughs along the way.

We named the book *Wit, Whimsy & Wisdom* to evoke a sense of what your devotional time will include. We divided the three-month guide into relevant sections. Feel free to read it straight through or choose what you need that day. Our sections feature:

- Worship & Prayer

- Humor

- Family

- Spiritual Growth

- Women's Issues

Before you dive in, I'd like to tell you how this book came about. Our writing group, WordGirls, spent time in 2020 improving our craft of writing devotions. We submitted our finished work to existing devotional publications and had a great response in receiving acceptance letters from editors. Yet, we felt God calling us to something more. A WordGirls devotional, designed to use God's Word and our words to help readers fall in love even more with the Word made flesh—Jesus.

During the process, we grew as individuals and as a group. We grew closer to God and closer to each other. I witnessed women helping each other, sacrificing their time to provide buddy edits for fellow writers. Women cheering on women—celebrating victories and coming alongside during struggles. Even though 2020 was a difficult year, this devotional project became a bright spot for us all. Now we pray, as we hand it off to our readers, that you too grow—and hopefully, you'll grin a little too!

Your WordGirlfriend,

Kathy Carlton Willis, WordGirls Founder
God's Grin Gal

About WordGirls

In 1994 I had a brainchild to start a group to coach fun, faith-filled women who were serious about the writing life. I served on faculty at national writers conferences and realized attendees remained stuck in the writing process. I'd see them come back year after year with their projects showing little progress. They were often overwhelmed by the conference material and didn't know how to apply it to their writing lives. They needed a group to keep them accountable and a coach to help them figure out their next steps.

I'm grateful to Deb DeArmond, who worked tirelessly with me through the launch process of this wonderful group of women. Her assistance and brainstorming helped me birth my vision for the group.

WordGirls is a special sisterhood of writing support for women who write from a biblical worldview (whether for the faith market or general market). We propel writers to the next level—regardless of where they are today.

Here's an overview of our exclusive WordGirls benefits:

1. Once-per-year, one-hour phone coaching to personalize your advancement as a writer and/or speaker.

2. Private Facebook group to interact, brainstorm, pray for each other, share ideas, ask questions, etc.

3. Monthly topics to help you grow as a writer. To enhance your learning, the topics will be covered through Facebook group discussions and Zoom live sessions (recorded for you to watch later if you can't make it live).

4. Downloadable PDFs offer extra training in the form of tutorials.

5. Weekly study hall. We designate a two-hour period to work on projects we call our B.I.C. time (butt in chair). Study hall provides added accountability.

6. Periodic challenges. Some challenges are month-long, and others last a season. These challenges will stretch you without overwhelming you. Guaranteed to increase productivity if you participate. (Participation is not required to be a member.)

7. Digital membership badge to post on your website or social media page.

8. Reduced rates for events and for-fee materials. We have online retreats and WordGirls@Home intensives. When safe to meet in person, we will also offer WordGirls Getaways again.

9. Opportunity to submit writing for our WordGirls publications.

10. Opportunity to hire our coach for a reduced hourly rate.

If you have questions, email me at kathy@kathycarltonwillis.com. To keep the group intimate, the WordGirls board will grant a limited number of memberships. We only have open enrollment two months per year: January (for a February to January membership period) and July (for an August to July membership period). The registration form can be found at:

kathycarltonwillis.com/wordgirls

We also open up the online and in-person retreats to non-members, so keep an eye on the website for details of upcoming events.

Worship
& Prayer

Hide and Seek

by Robin Steinweg

*"For the Son of Man came to seek
and to save the lost."*

LUKE 19:10 (ESV)

M Y FOUR-YEAR-OLD GRANDDAUGHTER has an inter-esting take on hide-and-seek. She tells me where she's going to hide, lets me know when she's gotten there, and a little voice reminds me where she is while I'm searching.

"I'm under the table right next to you, Gigi!"

When I discover her, she squeals and screams, uncomfortable and a teensy bit afraid to be found. But once I fold her in my arms, she clings tight and begs for a snuggle and a story. How I delight in her!

It seems hide-and-seek has been around quite some time. Adam and Eve had a daily stroll with the Lord God in the cool of the evenings. But after they sinned, their fellowship with him was broken. More than uncomfortable, they were actually afraid to face him. They hid, though he knew exactly where they were and why. It probably wasn't long before they missed the walks and fel-lowship they'd had. But with their eyes opened to evil, they knew they had blown it. They couldn't stand in the presence of perfect holiness.

I've had sweet times of fellowship, worship, and conversation with my Lord. Though maybe only a glimmer of what Adam and Eve had, I've walked with him in intimate closeness. But when I give in to temptation and allow sin to build a wall between us—whether I lose my temper, entertain a bad attitude, grumble and complain, or whatever it might be—I avoid my time with him. I'm uncomfortable and maybe a teensy bit afraid. It's my way of hiding. How silly! Like my granddaughter, I'm in plain view. My thoughts and actions aren't hidden from an omniscient God. When I finally come to him and confess, he folds me in his arms. I cling to him, comforted as he holds me. He forgives me. Our relationship is restored, and we delight in one another again.

The only hide-and-seek I want to play with my Lord is the kind that has me hidden with Christ in God. He's already found me.

Dear Lord, I come looking for you, wanting to be near you as I worship. I find, to my surprise, you are already coming to meet me. Thank you that you seek me, find me, and hide me in the safety of your love. I delight in you. Most amazing of all, you delight in me!

A "No More" List

by Sandy Lipsky

*He will wipe every tear from their eyes, and
there will be no more death or sorrow or crying
or pain. All these things are gone forever.*

REVELATION 21:4 (NLT)

HAVE YOU EVER felt as if you are drowning in grief? When my mom died, I kept asking God, "How do I do this grief thing?" The pain was so visceral, it was hard at times to catch my breath. Panic attacks were another unexpected manifestation of loss. Would joy ever return?

While crying out to God one morning, I heard a quiet answer to my question. Desperate for deliverance from this suffocating pain, I focused my attention on hearing God. His Spirit gently reminded me to thank him even in the storm. The verse in Revelation 21:4 interrupted my chaotic thoughts. In this passage of Scripture, the Lord states there will be no more death or sorrow or pain in heaven. What a wonderful promise! I began praising God for preparing a place in heaven for my mom. As I continued giving thanks, another thought formed. Make a personal *No More* list for Mom. I grabbed a notebook nearby, and the words flowed like a river after a bountiful rain.

- No more sin or fear or loss.

- No more surgeries and long recoveries.

- No more swollen ankles or shortness of breath.

- No more forgetting where you put things.

- No more relentless itching or sleepless nights.

Now, on days when I can't shake sorrow's shadow, I pull out my *No More* list. There are days I add to the list, and other times I simply read it. Remembering the goodness of God and his perfect provision comforts me. The light shining from these *No More* truths chases darkness away.

When I picture Mom with effortless breathing and walking sure-footed with slender ankles on streets of gold, a smile forms. Maybe joy hasn't left. Covered by grief for a time, it is beginning to shine through the sadness.

I miss my mom. God knew I would, so he sent me a reminder. A *No More* list.

Thank you, Father, for giving me a "No More" list. You are a God of promises who keeps his word. What comfort I find in this Revelation passage! May you be praised even amid the storms of life.

Joy in the Family of God

by Diana Leagh Matthews

━━━━━━●◉●━━━━━━

*May the God of hope fill you with all joy and
peace in believing, so that by the power of the
Holy Spirit you may abound in hope.*

ROMANS 15:13 (ESV)

D O YOU KNOW for sure where you'd spend eternity if today
were your last day?

Every Wednesday morning, I teach Bible study to the residents
at the nursing home where I work as the activities director. It is
the most anticipated activity of the week, even topping the ever-
popular bingo for many residents.

As we end the service each week, we sing a combination of
two songs by Bill and Gloria Gaither. Both discuss getting used to
and being part of the family of God. While these were foreign to
my residents in the beginning, they now heartily sing along and
even request the song occasionally at other times of the week.

Recently, I sat at the bedside of one resident as he prepared
to meet Jesus face to face. Taking his hand, I began to sing to
him. When I stopped, he opened his eyes and mouthed the word
"more." Once again, I began to sing and prayed I was not making
a mistake as I sang about the family of God.

I will never forget the glow that came over his sunken face as I sang to him about getting used to God's forever family. He emanated a peace—a joy—that radiated from the inside out and unlike anything I'd seen before.

It reminded me that as believers in Christ, we should all radiate this joy and peace. When others see Christ in us, they don't need to ask if we're believers. It is lived out in our actions. Sadly, I fail in this area as much as I succeed.

Do you overflow with joy and peace?

Lord, thank you for the reminder that once we come to you in faith, we are all part of the family of God. There are times when we don't feel like being joyful, and peace can't be found, but that is when we need to draw closer to you and other believers. Thank you for the reminder that one day we will spend eternity together. Until then, help us learn to love one another with love and joy that only come from you.

The Crying Lady in the Fifth Pew

by Edna Earney

───────●◉●───────

*He drew me up from the pit of destruction, out of the
miry bog, and set my feet upon a rock . . . He put a
new song in my mouth, a song of praise to our God.*

PSALM 40:2–3 (ESV)

WHY AM I crying? Why can't I stop? I didn't understand
my tears while I sang along with the congregation
again this Sunday. The choir director struck the downbeat with
his baton, the instrumentalists played, and the choir joined in. As
if on cue, my eyes welled up, and tears spilled down my cheeks. I
praised and worshipped.

This silent weeping continued for a couple of months while
attending a new church suggested by our marriage counselor. My
husband attended only the first two Sundays with me. He support-
ed my going but found the service too different from the church
he grew up in. It made him uncomfortable. But me? I felt right at
home. It seemed as though I had come *back* home, even though we
were in Southeast Texas and I had grown up in the northern pan-
handle, 650 miles away. My tears were cleansing, healing water to
my soul. Each week I experienced release. I was renewed. Revived.
Repentant. And I rejoiced.

Released from offenses I took on over the past years and wrongly blamed on my husband. We had both given up lucrative jobs, faced financial problems, and had forgotten how to communicate love to each other. Our marriage counselor suggested we try God!

Renewed in God's love for me and my love of him. I had ignored God for too long. His arms were still wide open, ready to welcome me home.

Revived to face another week with our toddlers as I worked from home for additional income, and my husband worked two jobs. Any young mother of little ones knows how tired she is at day's end. I added another three to four hours of typing at the end of the day. Did I mention I was sleep deprived?

Repentant for not seeking God's help earlier. Why did I think I could fix all the problems myself? I apologized to God.

Reflecting on that time, I know that my heavenly Father and the Holy Spirit worked in me, lifted me from the pit of despair, and set my course on a sure path to relationship with Christ. My tears were tears of release and restoration while God created a clean heart in me. I rejoiced, acknowledging God's loving care and guidance. And I still rejoice today, with a heart full of joy for a Redeemer God who patiently drew my husband to relationship with him, and to worship with me, just three years later.

My loving God, thank you for pulling me out of the pit, putting my feet on solid ground, and placing a new song in my heart.

You Don't Really Mean That

by Mary E. Curcio

*Then the Lord said to me, "You have seen well,
for I am ready to perform My word."*

JEREMIAH 1:12 (NKJV)

OUR SIXTH CHILD was soon to be born. I prayed for a boy since we had five girls. If we had a boy, though, where would we put him? Three daughters were in one bedroom and two in another. The smallest bedroom belonged to my husband and me.

We lived in a congested home in a congested village. Escaping to the country was a dream come true. I prayed for God's direction and then acted. We put the house on the market and waited for God to sell it.

We waited and waited and waited. Not one buyer came to see the house. The real estate agent worked diligently to sell our home. She said we lived in a bad section of town and would have difficulty getting an offer. I thought, "No wonder we had no buyers." I was so disappointed.

One day, a dear matriarch of our church stopped by. I dearly loved and respected her. Casually she asked, "How is the sale of the house going?"

I responded, "Not good. But if the Lord wants to sell it, he will, and if not, he won't."

"I don't think you mean that." Her wise words convicted my spirit.

After she left, I raced upstairs, anxious to get on my knees to pray. "Lord, if you want us to stay, we will. But if you'll sell our home, that would be great. Either way, I accept your will."

After praying, I shared my prayer with my husband. He looked astonished. He asked, "Do you really mean that?"

With true conviction, I said, "Absolutely."

That night, for the first time in weeks, I had peace.

The very next morning, I woke up to the phone ringing. It was my real estate agent, and she could barely speak. "Mary," she said. "We have a buyer. It's a cash sale, and you'll have to move in two weeks." My mind raced. Could we pack up five kids and a home in two weeks?

Looking back, I admit I was halfhearted about my prayer life. I learned that God wants us to mean what we say to him and to ourselves. Though he does not need our prayers to move him, our words are precious to him. When he heard my sincere prayer, that I was willing to lay down my dream of moving, he moved to answer my request.

Lord, forgive me for praying casual words. Thank you for showing me the truth about how I communicate with you and for answering my sincere prayers.

Surrounded by a Heavenly Host

by Joanie Shawhan

For He will give His angels [especial] charge
over you to accompany and defend and preserve
you in all your ways [of obedience and service].

PSALM 91:11 (AMPC)

*P*AIN RIPPED THROUGH my abdomen. Doubled over, I clutched my belly and stumbled. My friends chatted and laughed as I trailed them into the restaurant. They downed Mexican specialties. My fork lay untouched alongside an empty plate. I sipped my soda, hoping to stave off the queasiness triggered by pain.

Over the course of several months, the cramping during my cycle increased. Monthly ultrasounds revealed the ever-increasing size of my ovary, probably endometriosis, but cancer couldn't be ruled out. Finally, my doctor recommended surgery.

My breath caught in my throat. I'm not sure which terrified me more—the knife or the loss of control during anesthesia. Sometimes being a nurse is not advantageous. I knew about surgical pain and nausea from anesthesia, as well as every potential complication.

Once again, anxiety robbed my sleep. I heard a faint knock on my bedroom door. My housemate had seen the light peeking out under my door. She knew how helpless and frightened I felt, so she prayed for me.

As she prayed, a picture formed in my mind. I saw myself in the operating room, lying on a stainless-steel table bathed with light. As I scanned my surroundings, angels clad in flowing white gowns glowed. With folded wings, multiple angels had stationed themselves side by side along the four walls of the surgical suite. Their golden heads bowed. The ceiling could not accommodate their height. Each angel clasped the gilded handle of a sword. From hilt to point, the sword gleamed, its length extended from their chests to the floor.

At the head of the operating table, Jesus stood in a shining white gown, a sword in his hand.

Peace flooded me. I was no longer afraid. I knew I would be all right because a heavenly host surrounded me.

In the recovery room, though still groggy, I heard my doctor's voice. "We didn't find any cancer. You'll be fine."

Yes, I would be fine. God had sent his angels to protect me.

Twenty years later, I clung to this picture God had given me as an answer to prayer—a promise I desperately needed. This time, I faced surgery for ovarian cancer. Once again, his presence and angelic hosts surrounded and protected me. Though cancer was hard and chemotherapy even worse, I knew I would be fine.

Thank you, Lord, for protecting me, especially in those times I feel most vulnerable. When I feel helpless and afraid, remind me that you surround me with your love and peace, and sometimes you send your heavenly hosts.

Not My Will but Yours Be Done

by Joanie Shawhan

My soul is very sad and deeply grieved . . . My Father, if it is possible, let this cup pass away from Me; nevertheless, not what I will [not what I desire], but as You will and desire.

MATTHEW 26: 38–39 (AMPC)

"*I* HAVE STAGE FOUR bladder cancer," my sister said. "It's in my lungs and liver."

No! I groaned as I tightened my grip on the phone and grabbed the counter with my other hand. I felt as though I had been kicked in the chest with a force that sucked the oxygen out of my lungs. My heart broke for my sister and her family. Our family.

How could my go-to-the-gym-every-day sister have cancer? I Googled "bladder cancer," searching for some shred of hope, but I knew the grim prognosis. I had practiced oncology nursing far too long to don blinders.

Her diagnosis devastated me. How was I to pray?

One night in my darkened room, I heard a whisper in my spirit. "Walk her home."

I knew God had spoken. There would be no healing, no miracle for my sister. He was calling her home.

With tears streaming down my cheeks, I prayed. "Lord, give her more time."

Over the next five months, I prayed—for peace, relief from pain, closure, and God's presence and comfort. Even though she lived five hundred miles away, I asked God if I could be with her at the end.

On Good Friday, my birthday, the call came. My sister's condition had deteriorated. My sisters, Mom, and I drove in on Saturday. On Easter Sunday, we sat on the patio swing, soaked up the sun's rays, and chatted with my sister.

Monday morning, she was gone.

I was crushed. But Jesus understood. He had cried out to the Father, his tears mingled with drops of blood. Was there another way? Not my will, but your will be done.

This was not the path I would have chosen. Not the outcome I desired. But I'm grateful God answered my prayers. He gave my sister more time, extending the doctor's prognosis by several months. He also allowed me to be with her at the end.

In my grief, I cried out to God. He carried me through the pain of "not my will, but your will be done."

When painful circumstances break my heart, I thank you, Lord, for guiding me through the grief with your comforting presence.

Insomnia Intervention

by Eva Burkholder

*Don't worry about anything; instead, pray about everything.
Tell God what you need, and thank him for all he has
done. Then you will experience God's peace, which exceeds
anything we can understand.*

PHILIPPIANS 4:6–7 (NLT)

I AM A LIGHT sleeper, waking many times every night. I started wearing earplugs when I lived overseas because every sound disturbed me—the electricity going off or coming back on, critters running across the roof, cats tousling in the rafters, my husband snoring, or the night watchman banging on the metal pole outside my window to assure me of his protection. Throw in regular travel, jet lag, a variety of strange beds, and you have a recipe for insomnia.

By the time I reached middle age, my body revolted. Just as I'd begin to relax and get to that point of letting go, I'd jerk awake, heart pounding. Not surprisingly, I became anxious about falling asleep.

I forced my mind not to think about the fact that I lay awake. I did this by choosing to pray. I wrote verses about sleep on cards and read them before going to bed. This calmed me and kept my mind off trying to fall asleep. When I woke shortly after—because I did wake again—I offered quick prayers for family or church members. And as I told God my requests, I stopped worrying about how long I lay awake. Peace took over, and I drifted off—again.

While praying in order to fall asleep is not the best prayer strategy, it does fall under the Bible's instruction to "tell God what you need." And when I considered the original language of the writer, my sleep deprivation certainly qualified because this phrase implies the cry of a desperate soul lacking basic survival needs.

I still struggle with sleep. I continue to wake up many times a night, and the new challenges of my menopausal age aren't helping either. Whenever I wake up yet again from excessive heat, mounting decisions, concern for wayward loved ones, or simply the heaviness of the world, I tell God about it. Peace follows. And then an anxious thought comes again—and I hit repeat.

Some nights it takes many prayers and focused intention to calm my anxious heart, but I'm talking to God, and that counts, doesn't it?

What worries do you need to talk to God about?

Precious Jesus, I give you all my anxiety and concerns. I tell you what I need. Thank you for your greatness, power, love, kindness, generosity, and goodness, which enable me to trust that you will do exactly what I need and fill my heart with peace.

The Night the Coon Fell

by Charlaine Martin

*Therefore humble yourselves under the mighty hand
of God, that He may exalt you in due time, casting
all your care upon Him, for He cares for you.*

1 PETER 5:6–7 (NKJV)

*M*Y HUSBAND AND I finished building our house
recently—and we still love each other! It took longer than
usual since we constructed it ourselves. Over time, local wildlife
staked claim to it. Why not? After all, it was a great place to raise
their babies.

An Alberta Clipper swept in, forcing these critters to shelter
in our attic. One night, hoping to sleep well, we heard scampering
feet. These nuisances played tag all night. We got no sleep trying
to get them to no avail. Hubby set a small live trap, eventually
catching two young raccoons.

With eyes resembling those of our stowaways, we curled up
under the warm covers for a night's slumber. In the wee hours
of the morning—thump, thump, thump. We couldn't believe our
ears! These masked bandits had come to steal our much-needed
sleep. Desperate for shut-eye, my husband prayed loudly, "Lord,
please remove these creatures from our house. We can't continue

without sleep. Amen." I prayed along silently, so exhausted. The scampering sounds disappeared as we drifted off to sleep.

The next night—nothing. Grateful for one night's sleep, we thanked God for our rest. Oddly, we heard nothing more. Two days later, while doing yard work, I found a large raccoon lying beside our house. Dead. It must have fallen off the roof and hit its head. Stunned, I showed my husband. "Glory be! Thank you, Lord!" he shouted.

We rejoiced over God's answer to our prayers yet were sad about the coon's demise. Our teenaged grandson came over later, listening wide-eyed as we shared about God's answered prayer. God's miracle strengthened our faith and the faith of our grandson. God took care of what wreaked havoc in our lives.

Furry creatures tormented us, but in today's passage, the believers Peter addressed had *people* who persecuted them. Peter encouraged these Christians to take their concerns to God, who cares for them. God's people needed his intervention to strengthen their faith for the days ahead. Just as he answered their prayers, which bolstered their confidence, he answers our prayers today and shores up our confidence.

By taking our concerns to God, he addresses our pleas in ways that speak of his power and love. He thwarts what threatens to undo us. He also makes his mighty work evident that we might share it with others. Pray, giving God your problem with a grateful heart, knowing he cares for you. Thank him for his answer to your prayers and share it with others.

Thank you, Lord, for caring when situations trouble us. I am glad you invite us to bring them to you. When we leave our troubles at your feet, you address them, enabling us to be more effective for you. Thank you, Lord, that we can share your incredible works, drawing others to you.

On a Wing and a Prayer

by Sally Ferguson

---

*"For the LORD your God is living among you. He
is a mighty savior. He will take delight in you with
gladness. With his love, he will calm all your fears. He
will rejoice over you with joyful songs."*

ZEPHANIAH 3:17 (NLT)

*T*HE CABIN LIGHTS dimmed as passengers settled into their seats. It was quiet all around me, but inside, my heart cried, "Why?"

As I sat alone on the plane, I wondered, had it been only twenty-four hours earlier when my husband and I broached the subject of a flight to Florida? With his dad recovering from shoulder surgery, we knew Mom's care would be too much for my father-in-law. On the layover in Baltimore, Hubby texted, and I called to check in. The news was both shocking and dismal. The rehab center told his dad to call in hospice and make end-of-life preparations for his wife of fifty-seven years.

Now, overcome with memories of my mom-in-love, I didn't hold back the tears in that darkened plane. I looked across the empty seat and out over the tip of the wing, where the sky turned ablaze with vibrant hues of sunset. Red, orange, magenta, and colors more vivid than I'd ever seen bathed the horizon. But even more glorious were the songs that filled my heart. I began humming as words filtered through my mind. Hymns I hadn't heard in years were suddenly clear. God enveloped me in wonderful fellowship. I experienced sweet communion in the air, and my spirit felt hushed and full.

Why did the Lord surround me in those moments of serenity? Maybe he wanted to remind me he is sufficient for everything I face. Maybe he wanted to infuse me with peace before entering that caregiving season. Whatever the reason, it was a precious grace gift and a cherished leg of a trip into the unknown.

Lord, you are mighty and powerful. You save me in life's turmoil and quiet my fears. Thank you for singing over my life every day. I want to live in your presence and love.

Hidden Treasures of the Word

by Lisa-Anne Wooldridge

———●●●———

*Tune your ears to the world of Wisdom; set your
heart on a life of Understanding . . .
Searching for it like a prospector panning for gold,
like an adventurer on a treasure hunt.*

PROVERBS 2:2, 4 (MSG)

*H*AVE YOU EVER read a verse over and over because it didn't
seem to stick in your mind? Or have you read the Bible
and knew you gained knowledge, but you longed for a greater
connection to the words? Many times, I've read the Bible and felt
the scriptures come alive. Other days, to be honest, not so much.

So, what do you do on those days? Sometimes I switch gears
and listen to worship music. Sometimes I close my eyes to pray—
or nap—whichever comes first! I firmly believe Jesus napped, even
if the Father never sleeps!

Over the years, I've gleaned new ways of doing things that
work for me when I don't feel the connection. I know there are
untold riches hidden between the covers of the Bible, so I like to
think of myself as a treasure hunter in search of gold.

I've made myself a map, now, and it works every time. It's
pasted together with bits of insight from various friends, pastors,
and mentors. If you create a map, it won't necessarily look like

mine, but perhaps I'll have some of the missing pieces you need to find your own treasure.

First, I figure out where I am. This is the *You Are Here* part of the map. Is something bothering me or heavy on my mind? I deal with that first and then plant myself in the present.

Next, I prepare myself by resting for a moment or two in God's presence, letting stress, the need to perform, or any other weight fall off my shoulders. I simply breathe and enjoy the peace of time with him. It's always easier to hear his voice in the Bible when you are aware of his presence with you and in you.

Now I'm ready to find the living Word in the ancient text. This is the *X Marks the Spot* part of the map. I usually follow this path from Lectio Divina: read, reflect, respond, and rest.

- **Read.** Sometimes less is more. Watch for anything that stands out—a word or a phrase that God highlights to me.

- **Reflect.** Meditate on that word. Ask God to illuminate it for me.

- **Respond.** Thank God for the Scripture and pray through it with him. Listen for anything he might be leading me to do or understand in this passage and write it down.

- **Rest.** My favorite part. Take whatever God speaks to me through his Word and store it up in my heart. Add it to my treasure chest. Then I rest in gratitude and love until I'm ready to take the treasure and carry it with me into my day.

Thank you for the treasures in your Word, Lord.
Seal them in my heart forever.

A Cup of Grace

by Darla S. Grieco

———◦●◦———

*And we know that for those who love God all
things work together for good, for those who are
called according to his purpose.*

<small>ROMANS 8:28 (ESV)</small>

T HE SWEET, BUBBLY coffee barista I'd come to know and love stuck her head out of the drive-thru window. "Your drink'll be up in a minute, but I have some bad news."

Bad news, for me? I couldn't imagine. Were they out of cups?

"Tomorrow is my last day," Josie continued.

"Aw, we will miss you," I assured her. "But that's exciting for you, right? What do you have planned?"

She propped her chin on her arm. "I don't really know. I just know it's time to leave the food service industry. They offered a separation package, so I took it. I think I'd like to go into office work. Business administration maybe."

A coworker handed her my drink, which she, in turn, passed to me. Meanwhile, my mind started performing calisthenics. *Was she serious?* Less than twelve hours prior, I sent a prayer request to my Bible study friends: "I need the Lord to send me office help. I do not know how or where to even advertise these days or what type of position we need. But I'm overwhelmed, and simply cannot do it alone any longer."

Was this young lady an answer to my prayer?

I slid my coffee into its holder and turned back to Josie.

"So, you have no plans at all?"

"I'm thinking about going back to school. But no, I'm not sure."

"Well, it just so happens we are creating an administrative position at our office. We could use help. If you'd like to give me your number, I'll send you more information when we post the job. I'd be happy to look at your resume."

Josie's eyes grew wide. "Sure!" she exclaimed.

She fumbled for a piece of paper to share her number with me.

"I'll be in touch," I promised.

We never did post that job. Why would we? God always has better plans.

Ten days later, Josie joined our team at the office as an administrative assistant. I explained to her how she had been an answer to my prayers. She immediately confided that the night before sharing her parting news with me, she also prayed for God to show her what she should do next. "I had no idea where I was going to go or what I would do, but I knew it was time to leave and had to trust God for the rest."

Lord, thanks for reminding me that you can do abundantly more than I hope or imagine. May I always turn to you instead of depending upon myself. Your plans are much greater.

Wordless Sighs and Aching Groans

by Gina Stinson

*God's Spirit is right alongside helping us along. If we
don't know how or what to pray, it doesn't matter. He
does our praying in and for us, making prayer out of our
wordless sighs, our aching groans.*

ROMANS 8:26 (MSG)

FOLLOWING MY FATHER'S death, I remember sitting in
my dorm room at Bible college wanting to pray—to pour
my heart out to God. I was at a loss for words. I thumbed through
my Bible, hoping for a verse to jump out. As I flipped through the
pages, a piece of paper fluttered to the ground with Romans 8:26
written on it. I recalled someone had slipped it in my hand the day
of the funeral. Finding it this particular day was a game-changer
for me.

I was released. I no longer had to be the church girl with all
the answers. I didn't have to pretend everything was wonderful.
My heart and my head could finally agree. I didn't have to understand or have the words. Someone else could do that for me.

Finding myself in a similarly distraught time in my life, I
returned to the verse again in August of 2002, when my daughter
was born thirteen weeks early. This time, in a tiny eight-by-eight-
foot waiting room reserved for parents of NICU babies, I tried

unsuccessfully to pray alone. I tried at her tiny incubator bed, with my husband, with friends, at church—but my heart never had the right words to say. And it was okay. Someone else could do that for me.

Now, over eighteen years later, I've grown accustomed to letting my intercessor, the Holy Spirit, pray those difficult prayers. The ones we pray when death is near, when cancer calls, when there is loss, when finances are failing. It comforts me to know a God who can interpret the very groanings of my heart. When words don't come easy, His Spirit intercedes and interprets those deep, tender, anxious words our mouths can't seem to utter. Someone else can do that for me.

Maybe you're like me and sometimes try to force conversation with God. Quite possibly, you've experienced what I've felt in those dark, desolate moments. Remember, we don't need to know what to say, how to say it, or even when to say it. He hears those cries, those moments of unimaginable pain and anguish. He knows. He will carry our cries to Father God.

He will do that for you and me.

Like a good father, Lord, you see me when I am hurting. You know what I am trying to communicate before it even leaves my lips. Thank you for providing your Spirit to translate those feelings into prayers. Thank you for your extravagant love that wants to hear from me—even at my lowest.

Redirect

by Gina Stinson

Why am I discouraged? Why is my heart so sad?
I will put my hope in God! I will praise him
again—my Savior and my God!

PSALM 42:11 (NLT)

WATCHED AS MY son waddled his way toward the television. His saggy diaper was the only thing hindering him from a full-on sprint. He had learned to crawl one week, and within just a few more weeks, he was up and running. Our world was about to become a maze of baby gates and high reaches. This kid was on the move.

Most of the time, I turned him around to go in a different direction when he headed toward something dangerous. Other times, I used my "mom voice," shouted a firm, "No!" and he turned away. And sometimes, if he went too far, he received a light pat on the rear or the hand, reminding him to listen and obey.

He quickly learned the art of redirection.

Redirection isn't a new toddler training technique. It's been around for ages. The beauty of redirecting is the new view you take in when your focus changes. Redirecting my attention when I am in a dangerous or difficult place helps me focus on what is worth my attention. We are guaranteed to have trouble in this world. But the psalmist tells us, in an instant with the right redirect, we can praise and worship our Savior and God.

I recently attended a funeral where, during the middle of one of the songs, the sister-in-law of the deceased stood in worship to God. By her stance, she testified to the entire congregation that she believed in a God who was in control and worthy of worship. One by one, others in the crowd rose to their feet. Her example of worship overflowed in that space.

When we redirect our pain, hurt, and worries, we give room for God to be worshipped and glorified. Just like how my son learned to recognize my tone when he needed to redirect, we can tune our ears to listen for opportunities to worship every day. We don't have to wait for hard times, but it sure is reassuring to know, even then, we can redirect our thoughts to an amazing God and worship.

Lord, thank you for giving me the ability to redirect my thoughts from my circumstances to the hope I have in you. Help me turn my heart toward you and focus on you as savior and God.

How Beautiful

by Kathy Carlton Willis

*Happy are those who hear the joyful call
to worship, for they will walk in the
light of your presence, Lord.*

Psalm 89:15 (nlt)

WHEN PRAISE SONGS sing of Christ's splendor, the words draw me in. I imagine how beautiful Jesus must have been while on this earth and how magnificent he is to me today. It is the same when I am drawn to a beautiful Christian. Their radiant glow (which must be reflecting the beauty of Christ) is what attracts me. Physical features fade in comparison. I want to be with a person who cherishes the Lord in a personal way!

I think this is what also captivates and invites me to Jesus. He is the one who can bring me to the Father. While on this earth, he stayed completely focused on the will of the Father. He kept his purpose ever in focus—his special design. I gravitate toward believers who know what God wants for their lives, those willing to sacrifice everything else to pursue godly direction.

How beautiful is the sweet glow of mercy on the face of Jesus. How special are the arms held open wide to welcome me to his side. How piercing are his eyes, penetrating me with his love and understanding. The mouth of Jesus shares both laughter and smiles of contentment. His words beckon me.

I desire to worship Jesus in all of his beauty. We often forget how to truly worship. May we make our adoration known to him. We must not hold back for fear of intimacy! Only when we draw near to God can we know him. When new friends in Christ attract us because of their inner beauty, we drop our walls of inhibition to really know them and be known by them. Equally so, to truly seek Jesus, it takes throwing aside any weight that hinders our journey so we can run to him.

I can scarcely fathom what it will be like when I see my Savior face to face. How overjoyed I will be, yet how humbled! I am determined not to wait for my heavenly graduation to worship Jesus with abandon.

As I come into your presence, I worship you. Oh, how beautiful you are to me! You are high and lifted up. May I radiate your shine so others are drawn to an intimate relationship with you.

Delight of My Heart

by Mindy Cantrell

—————●◉●—————

Your words were found, and I ate them, and your
words became to me a joy and the delight of my heart,
for I am called by your name, O Lord, God of hosts.

JEREMIAH 15:16 (ESV)

WHEN I AM down, when I am grieving, when I am in distress, O Lord, I turn to you and find your words. I meditate on them, and I eat them. I speak them and pray them out loud, and they are a balm to my soul.

In the midst of despair, O Lord, I trust in you. I cry out to you, and there you are with me! You speak softly to me your words of comfort, and I hear you. You take my hand and lead me out of darkness into your light of hope. For you, O Lord, have rescued me, and you call me by my name.

When I am happy, when I am celebrating, when I have joy, O Lord, I do not forget you. I find your words and eat them and meditate on them. I pray them out loud in thanksgiving and praise, and they are the celebration of my soul!

When I am in awe, when I praise, when I worship, I feel your presence most keenly. Your love washes over me, touching me, filling me with the knowledge that you are right there with me. I am not alone. I find your words and sing them and pray them out loud to you as I surrender my will to yours. For you, O Lord, are always with me, leading me, loving me, and keeping me safe. You are forever my Lord and Savior, and I will joyfully lift my heart to you. As I eat your faithful words, they are the salvation of my soul.

Wherever I am, whatever I'm doing, I understand that I am loved and wanted for all time. I find your lifegiving words of love and affirmation, and I eat them. I speak and pray them out loud, over my life, my body, my soul, and they are healing to my wounds—the joy and delight of my heart!

Dear heavenly Father, may I always see and look to you as the comfort and balm to my grieving soul. May I always call upon you and trust you to rescue me in times of trial and despair. And, Father, may I always remember to praise you in times of celebration, as I lift my heart to you and treasure you as my salvation.

Humor

Nurture with Neglect

by Robin Steinweg

*Consider it a sheer gift, friends, when tests and challenges
come at you from all sides. You know that under pressure,
your faith-life is forced into the open and shows its true colors.*

JAMES 1:2–3 (MSG)

I HAD NO IDEA I could actually kill with kindness.

See, I have this thing for blue flowers. Not the bluish-tinted purple or lavender that the seed companies like to name as if they really are blue. I prefer the honest-to-goodness true blue flowers. The ones with hues like a summer sky or like water reflecting that sky. Heavenly Blue morning glories are just that kind of blue. I've tried over the years to grow them from seed, but they've never gotten large enough to produce blooms.

One spring, the local hardware store had some of the plants in its greenhouse. They were vigorous, already climbing up a skinny stake. I bought one and carefully packed shopping bags around it to keep it from toppling over. At home, I found a sunny location and gave it the best soil. A week later, when it resumed its ascent, I rejoiced. By summer's end, I was going to have the biggest blue blossoms ever.

I babied that morning glory. Plucked every threatening weed, fed it regularly, and spoke encouraging words to it. (Hey, don't

A WORDGIRLS COLLECTIVE: HUMOR   37 judge me! They say plants can use the carbon dioxide from our breath.)

And so it went through June and July. In August, I began to gloat over the healthy vine climbing an antique (well, old and defunct) ladder. In September, I took pictures of it. Twelve feet tall, with lush, thick leaves that could screen celebrities from paparazzi. But still, nary a bloom nor even a bud.

Experienced gardeners, I'm sure, are shaking their heads, already aware of the problem. I finally looked it up online: Why aren't my morning glories blooming? Why is their glory hiding? What did I neglect?

Neglect!

For morning glories to produce bodacious blue blooms, they require poor soil. Harsh conditions. Instead, I coddled them with fertilizer the entire summer, denying them the thing I never imagined they needed—neglect.

My heavenly Father, Master Gardener, knows when to feed one of his tender shoots, when to protect it, and when to give it a support to climb. He knows when a certain amount of hardship—what we might view as neglect—will make his precious vine fulfill its purpose and flower freely.

My kind Lord, the next time I face hardship or a trial, help me to remember that your love for me is unfailing. You know exactly what I need and when I need it to bloom and bear the fruit of your Spirit. Help me to be patient and trust you.

Trust Me (Wink)

by Robin Steinweg

*And those who know your name put their
trust in you, for you, O Lord, have not
forsaken those who seek you.*

PSALM 9:10 (ESV)

"*L*ET ME GET this straight. You want me to stand up on this table, fall backward, and trust six or so giggling teenagers to catch me? And you're telling me this illustrates our trust in God?"

The teen Sunday school class had gone on the prowl for some unsuspecting vict—I mean, participant. I was on my way to the choir room when they found me. I searched my brain for any excuse. My high school gymnastics coach once dropped me, even though she'd been trained to catch people. My fear of heights made high heels seem too tall. Mom taught me never to put my feet on a table.

I looked at their eager faces. What could I say? They hauled me up onto the table, and down I dropped, praying for safety. By some miracle, they caught me. Their experiment was a success. I didn't tell them how many bruises I counted the next day. They never knew how carefully, from then on, I made sure not to be nabbed by any more Sunday school classes.

I'm not sure what the teens learned that day. As for me, I came away thinking it was a poor illustration. After all, the important thing is not the trust—it's *who* we're trusting. If God had said to me, "Fall off this table into my arms, child," I'd have had no problem.

Or would I?

Maybe the real test is believing God is able to work even through faulty human beings. It's knowing that even if I end up with bruises, he'll work it out for my good. It isn't only trusting him when I choose to and am in control of the circumstances. It's also when I must place myself in someone else's hands—the dentist, the doctor—even some teens.

Lord, I admit it's hard for me to let go and trust you.
It's a little like falling backward into the air, hoping to be
caught. Help me to do better.

Bark, Please

by Robin Steinweg

So let's not get tired of doing what is good. At just the right time we will reap a harvest of blessing if we don't give up.

GALATIANS 6:9 (NLT)

*T*HE FRONT DOOR stood open a few inches. I knew I'd locked it that morning. As we returned after dark, our son saw someone sneak past the living room window, hunched over. I'd already pulled into the garage but backed out and called 911. From a safe distance, we watched two police officers enter our shadowy house with guns drawn.

They came out with good news. Nobody there, nothing appeared harmed. We didn't detect anything missing. How could we avoid this in the future? Have a locksmith rekey the locks and get a dog, they said. Barking dogs are a great deterrent to intruders.

At the humane shelter, Buddy sat politely in the midst of the other dogs' frenzied barking, gazing at us. We brought home our canine alarm system.

But Buddy didn't bark. I was determined to train him. How does someone train a dog to bark?

They bark.

I barked. Buddy and our boys watched. When I'd barked

enough, I gave myself a treat (cookie). If Buddy even looked as if he was interested, I gave him a treat (bone). I barked daily. Weekly. Monthly. I barked myself hoarse. We went through boxes of expensive treats for people and treats for dogs with no sign of progress. I felt mighty foolish barking when there really was someone at the door. But I didn't want my sons to see me give up. I wanted them to learn perseverance. I also wanted the dog to bark.

Finally, Buddy's lip twitched. I praised and petted him. When his lip curled, I praised him more. When he snorted a bit as his lip curled, I fawned over him. Eventually, he vocalized the tiniest bit. I went nuts. When he finally did bark, I rolled over, howled, sat up—did everything but play dead. He knew he'd done something great. And he kept on doing it. A couple of weeks later, we had to train him to quit barking.

Someone has said, "The race is not always to the swift, but to those who keep on running." What do you face today that you're tempted to abandon? "Keep your eyes on Jesus, who both began and finished this race we're in. Study how he did it. Because he never lost sight of where he was headed" (Hebrews 12:2 MSG).

*Lord, make me like the little nut who held its
ground—and became an oak.*

Fling It Far

by Darla S. Grieco

I perceived that there is nothing better for them than to be joyful and to do good as long as they live.

ECCLESIASTES 3:12 (ESV)

ONE SPRING, I escorted my daughter for a three-day field trip to the mountains with our school district. Fifth graders from all the elementary schools converged for team-building activities such as canoeing and maneuvering through obstacle courses, hoping they'd meet new friends for their transition to middle school. As chaperones, the parents maintained a tight schedule and ensured everyone's safety.

Naturally, I took my responsibilities seriously. Until I reached Dr. Brecht's station. "Everyone, line up here on the edge of the field," she commanded.

Everyone? No way. I beelined for the wooden benches off to the side and assumed a proper ladylike position. Legs crossed. Hands on knees.

"Excuse me." I heard a sing-songy voice coming from the field. "You, over there."

Pointing at my chest, I gave her a perplexed expression.

She summoned with a wagging finger. "Come on."

She couldn't be serious. I'm a mother. We sit on the sidelines. We don't play.

I realized I was fighting a losing battle, so I joined the others.

"Now, everyone, untie one shoe. Right. Left. I don't care. Your goal is to fling your shoe off your foot farther than anyone else."

I stood, mouth agape. *Was this woman insane? What was I to do once I released my shoe? I'd be standing in a field with only one shoe on.*

Hives crept up my neck. I looked longingly toward my bench. But it was too late.

Shoes were flying off feet, one after the next. The children laughed and cheered, their energy and excitement invigorating my spirit. I fought tears that threatened to spill from my eyes as a new emotion I hadn't felt in a long time began to surface. *Was that joy?*

For ten years, I'd played the role of a parent—a serious, uptight parent. Where had that gotten me? I had a decision to make.

With one sneaker dangling on the edge of my toes, I clunked back two steps. Hunkering down, I raced toward the kicking line. I swung my leg with all my might and watched as my shoe soared up and outward, spinning through the air. Joy swelled inside me.

That felt amazing!

I watched my shoe hit the ground, take a bounce, and tumbled just beyond the group's record kick.

"We have a new winner!" shouted Dr. Brecht.

I realized I had behaved for years as I thought I should instead of how God created me to be—a playful Christian woman who experiences joy and flings it outward for all to receive.

Later by the campfire, Dr. Brecht awarded me Shoe Flinging Champion of our team.

I still have the certificate for proof.

Lord, help me to remember that while discipline and order have their place, so does enjoying life. May you help me find joy even in the little things.

Hanging with the White Horse

by Edna Earney

*I saw heaven opened, and behold, a white horse! The one sitting
on it is called Faithful and True . . . And the armies of heaven,
arrayed in fine linen . . . were following him on white horses.*

REVELATION 19:11, 14 (ESV)

*H*AVE YOU EVER watched your pups having a dream? I
watched Dickens, our little Shih Tzu, "sleep running" in
bed and envisioned him recounting his eventful night. My imagination resulted in this narration from his point of view.

ↄ

I heard the missus reading bedtime stories to the red-headed
little ones last night about animals in the Bible. They giggled
and leaned closer to see the pictures. She prayed with them, then
called, "Dickens. Come on, buddy," and we went to bed. As soon
as I curled up at her feet, I started dreaming about the animals in
the stories.

First, I saw Balaam beating his donkey. I felt so sad. Then the
angel of the Lord gave the donkey the ability to talk (Numbers
2:28). I panted and barked as I remembered the little ones
laughing at the man. He must have been so surprised when his
donkey talked back! *Way to go, donkey!* Sometimes I bark and bark,
trying to get the mister and missus to understand me. Wouldn't

it be wonderful to be able to use their language to get them to understand? Sometimes a dog just wants some steak added to his dinner bowl!

Then I dreamed about the tired donkey at the stable where baby Jesus was born. Coming in with the shepherds, I saw the baby and decided to stand guard. Everyone was in awe, but they kept their distance. They saw my ears pulled back—no one was going to threaten that little one! I barked to the donkey, "You can rest now from your trip." I glanced at the manger, and the calm baby looked straight at me, eyes unmoving. I think he was saying, "Good job, Dickens!" I wagged my tail.

Then I got excited! I saw a white horse, followed by armies on white horses. The armies were dressed in white linen, so I fit right in with my white fur. The lead horse snorted and stamped, ready for battle. *I'm ready too! I'm going to run beside the white horse!* And the one called Faithful and True looked around, caught my eye, then gave the signal. "Charge!"

My legs ran harder than ever—panting—running—*huh?* The missus was patting me and whispering, "Wake up!" *I must have been bunching up the bedsheets.*

That was a good dream. I licked my tired paws. *Did the little ones dream about animals too?* Time to go nuzzle them awake and find out!

Father God, thank you for understanding me, no matter what language I speak. And thank you for finding so many creative ways to capture my attention and speak to me. Help me listen with open ears and an open heart.

WIT, WHIMSY & WISDOM

Toolbars, Widgets, and Docks, Oh My!

by Joanie Shawhan

———•——•——•———

*Now thanks be to God who always leads
us in triumph in Christ.*

2 Corinthians 2:14 (NKJV)

STARED AT THE darkened computer screen. What do I do now?

A diagnosis of ovarian cancer pushed me to purchase my first laptop—a Mac.

I had recently learned the basics of email and Google on the PCs at work. Would my minimal knowledge translate into operating my new computer? I hoped so. It would be my lifeline to the outside world while I endured several months of chemotherapy.

"Would you like the three-year warranty?" the clerk asked. "It includes three years of free technical phone support."

Three years of phone support? "Sign me up!"

Armed with *Mac for Dummies*, I embarked on this technological quest. First step, find the browser—Safari. I laughed. I needed the courage of the cowardly lion to face the jungle hiding in this motherboard.

"Locate Safari in the dock," I read. *Dock? Isn't that where one moors a boat?* With my mind fuzzy from the chemotherapy drugs,

I chugged through my search engine. I meticulously followed the instructions but failed to find a dashboard, bookmarks, or icons.

What's a toolbar? Computer language, foreign to me, collided with my chemo brain, spinning my neurons into a state of freeze tag. In my frustration, a more appropriate tool in my toolbar might have been a hammer.

I resorted to technical phone support.

"What is your operating system?" the technician asked. "Click the apple in the upper left corner."

He instructed. I clicked. After about an hour, I was stuck. He requested a screen share. *Does that mean he can see me?* I knew my computer was equipped with a camera. I shuddered, noting my faded pajamas and shining bald head, courtesy of chemotherapy. Laying aside my pride, I allowed the technician control of my screen. His gray arrows surfaced like random ghosts. I clicked each arrow as we managed widgets, set up my email, contact information, bookmarks, and keychain.

Two hours later, I was on my own, armed and dangerous with the little knowledge I had gleaned.

I wish I could say I hadn't required further phone support. But when I realized the technician could only view the screen and not me, I laughed at my overactive imagination and added the number to speed dial.

I'm still not tech savvy, but little by little, I've grown in my computer skills with a confidence I'd never thought possible.

Some tasks seem insurmountable. But equipped with patience and perseverance, I've learned that with God's help, I can become proficient at a new skill if I tackle the project one step at a time. I cannot say I've mastered my computer, but I press forward. He helps me succeed.

Thank you, Lord, for encouraging me and giving
me the confidence to learn new skills. And
providing help when I get stuck.

I Didn't Sign Up for This!

by Joanie Shawhan

———◦◉◦———

*The Lord God is my Strength . . . He makes my feet like hinds'
feet and will make me to walk . . . and make [spiritual] progress
upon my high places [of trouble, suffering, or responsibility]!*

HABAKKUK 3:19 (AMPC)

GRIPPED BY THE fear of heights, I clutched at tree limbs
for support as I clawed my way up the bluff's craggy face.
Panting, I heaved my ample *derriere* over the uneven boulders.
Loose pebbles rattled and plunged down the cliff, crashing onto
the bed of jagged quartzite rocks below. I didn't sign up for this.
One slip, and I could die today. *Please help me, God.*

Thirty minutes earlier, my brother had surveyed the first few
feet of the irregularly shaped stepping-stone trail that loomed before us. The rest of the path lay hidden, shrouded in foliage. "This
doesn't look so bad," he mumbled. "We can always turn back."

My brother lied.

I hoisted my leg and stepped up onto the rock my brother
had just scrambled over. I teetered and tumbled backward. Our
eyes met in terror as I reached for his outstretched hand. But I
grasped only air. My backside slammed into a boulder. Stunned, I
dusted myself off and crawled up the rock-strewn trail. No turning
back now.

Tears spilled down my cheeks and mingled with the sweat that dripped from my brow. Suddenly, I doubled over a rock as giggles burst forth. *Why was I laughing?*

Even though my circumstances hadn't changed, I felt a new strength surge through my frayed nerves and throbbing muscles. I recognized the joy as a gift from God. Joy giving me the strength and courage I needed to overcome the obstacles of climbing the bluff (which we dubbed The Cliffs of Insanity).

Sometimes when trials overwhelm me, I feel as if I'm scaling cliffs of insanity. I want to tell God, "I didn't sign up for this!" I begin to doubt his goodness and faithfulness because my circumstances don't line up with my view of a loving God.

But God hasn't changed. He is still with me. He not only helps me but cheers me on to triumph over life's obstacles.

Clambering The Cliffs of Insanity made me stronger—not only physically but emotionally and spiritually. My self-talk changed from "I can't do this!" to "I overcame because God enabled me." I experienced a new level of trust in God and a sense of joy in accomplishing what seemed impossible.

*Lord, thank you for strengthening me when I reach
the end of my physical and emotional stamina. You
protect me and enable me to climb heights I never
thought possible. You gift me with joy.*

Avoiding Bollards

by Eva Burkholder

*Not that we are sufficient of ourselves to think
of anything as being from ourselves, but our
sufficiency is from God.*

2 CORINTHIANS 3:5 (NKJV)

A ROW OF BOLLARDS loomed in front of me. My heartbeat accelerated. My cadence slowed. The bike path was challenging enough without the prospect of navigating between a row of narrowly placed poles. These fixed posts, designed to keep vehicles from crossing, threatened to disrupt my peaceful ride with my husband. I tentatively approached the menacing structures, certain I would hit one. With careful attention, I wobbled through.

I breathed a sigh of relief. My confidence rose. I pedaled on and started to enjoy myself until I saw another row of bollards. *You can do this*, I told myself. *No problem.* Gulping air, I plowed ahead, crashed right into one, and fell off my bike. Yes, my husband laughed at me.

I decided I don't like bollards—even though I like the sound of the word. If there might be more of them, I wanted to quit bike riding altogether. Why was I so afraid of a short metal post?

My fear surprises me. I regularly speak in front of large groups of people and fly halfway around the world with ease. But bollards force me to think about situations I avoid. I don't travel in a busy city unless someone else takes the wheel. I send emails instead of making phone calls. I have to acknowledge that my avoidance is actually fear.

Left to my own willpower, I would keep my boundaries restricted. Recognizing my small fear of bollards gives me a way to start standing up to larger ones. But, I don't have to do this alone. The Bible says my sufficiency, my power, and my competency is from God, not me. Therefore, I will depend on his power to give me what I need to tackle my fears and not shy away from them.

What are you afraid of? Being alone? Intimacy? Loss of control? Pain? Rejection? What might you miss because you are avoiding facing that fear?

Lord God, empower me with your sufficiency to face my fears and not avoid them. I praise you and trust that you are big enough to walk with me through my fear. Help me stand and face it and take the next step.

Location! Location! Location!

by Lisa-Anne Wooldridge

*"'In him we live and move and
have our being.'"*

WHERE I LIVE in sunny, friendly Northern California—where the mountains meet the redwoods, and the redwoods meet the sea—the real estate market is always hopping. In fact, it seems that everyone wants to live here, which explains why there are six million people in my backyard.

There are a lot of perks for living here, from job opportunities to weather to outdoor beauty. But there are drawbacks, too, from the cost of living to crowds to crime. Sometimes I feel as if I've landed in paradise, and sometimes I'd give anything to live on a small country road in the back of beyond. I'm not sure what I'd do there, but there would be chickens and an herb garden, you can count on that!

Do you ever feel that sense of wishing to be somewhere—anywhere—else? The desire to pack a bag and take off for parts unknown? Sometimes I daydream about starting over with a fresh slate in a new town where nobody knows my name. My cat is giving me a worried look right now. I hope she isn't a mind-reader!

I have an aunt who insists I have "itchy feet" because I wandered so far from my childhood home. It's true. I've lived all over, and I've loved each new place. But still, some part of me is always longing for somewhere else.

For years, I thought perhaps I was afraid to grow where I was planted, or perhaps I wasn't thankful enough for the situations where God placed us. I worried about not being content with what God had provided in that season. I worried even more when I realized we'd be moving to the "foreign land" of California. I'd heard jokes about California my entire life. It was "the granola state"—full of fruits, flakes, and nuts. I wasn't sure what to expect, but I was on the lookout for muesli!

When I moved to California, I found my people. One of them, a wonderful older woman who'd been a real Jesus People hippie back in the day, gave me the wisdom I was missing.

"Obviously, you're never going to be content with where you live on this planet. This world is not your home." Then she added, "Don't just wait for heaven. Realize where you are now! To find contentment, remember who is in you, and who you're in! It's all about location. Think about what you have here and now. Anywhere you move, you are *in* Christ."

Her words calmed my heart and my itchy feet, too. For a quarter of a century now, I've been blooming where I was planted. I tell people I live in the land of cashew milk and honey, which goes just perfectly with crunchy granola!

Jesus, open our eyes to see that we abide in you, and there is no place like home.

What Not to Wear

by Gina Stinson

*Put on the whole armor of God, that you may
be able to stand against the schemes of the devil.*

EPHESIANS 6:11 (ESV)

I WAS IN THE sixth grade—fully embracing the awkward
stage of braces, glasses, and a bad haircut.

Hankering for something different to wear, I ventured to my
mom's closet. It was full of things—beautiful things. On the day I
tiptoed to her room while she was out of town and my dad was at
work, I soaked in the unique accessories, bright colors, and smells
of leather and perfumes. I determined to wear one of her dresses to
school the next day.

I spotted the grey outfit with small pink flowers and puffed
sleeves. It had a lightweight matching vest sewn to the front and
a soft, pleated skirt. It was one of my favorite dresses. I knew this
was *the one*. I snatched it from the rack and scrambled to my room.

The next morning, outfitted in Mom's glorious garment, I
loaded into the car. My dad didn't even give me a second glance!
How could he not notice that it was too big? How could he not
remember seeing my mom wearing it? I have no idea. I went to my
sixth-grade class proudly wearing my mom's dress that day. I felt

as sophisticated as Mom when she wore it. Looking back, I realize how ridiculous I must have appeared. I wonder what my teachers must have thought.

Silly, huh? But as I thought of this story today, I realized that as a Christian woman living in the modern world, it is foolish to think I can go into the world's closet and wear its garments and no one will notice. We think, *it's just a day, it's just one dress, it's just a trip to school and back.* But the world is watching much more closely than my dad. Desiring to deceive us, the Enemy convinces us to put on pride, anger, bitterness, or any other attitudes or actions that might temporarily appear justified.

The truth is, we look ridiculous clothed in garments that weren't made for us. We become the hypocrites, the laughingstock, the poster child for what not to wear.

Because I know Christ, I want to look and behave differently. It can't happen if I am dressed like the world. It takes an intentional effort to wear the clothes that were made to fit me perfectly—a garment of praise, the armor of God, and righteousness. And no matter how cute, perfect, or just my size they might look at the moment, pride, anxiousness, or a bad attitude look can stay on my what-not-to-wear list.

Lord, help me to put on the garments you have made for me. Help me to discard the filthy rags that the Enemy has tried to entice me to wear. Thank you for helping me look more like you each day.

God-Beauty

by Mindy Cantrell

───────●◉●───────

*Those who look to him are radiant, and their
faces shall never be ashamed.*

PSALM 34:5 (ESV)

*E*VER HAD ONE of those awful, turn-your-face-red, life-em-
barrassing moments? Me too, and—true confession—more
than one. Here's my latest.

To preface, I'm a Texas girly girl with below-the-shoulder,
lightly layered hair. I have worked hard to create an updated version of the big hair sensation. To get this big hair perfection re-
quires a bit (okay, maybe a lot) of precise teasing here and there
and a liberal application of hairspray.

So, yesterday I worked up my big hair masterpiece and went
for some long-awaited shopping. Woohoo!

As I browsed through glorious racks of marked-down treasures, I noticed people staring at me, some almost laughing! *What
in the world?* I know some people think my big Texas hair is silly,
but they don't usually laugh. So, I worked my way to the ladies'
room and looked in the mirror. *Oh, dear Lord!*

Sticking out of the side of my head was a perfect mass of rat-
ted up, sprayed stiff, nest of hair! It looked like a little alien peeking

out, nodding to passersby as I moved. No wonder I became the spotlight exhibit in this fine store.

Mortifying? Yes. Self-confidence sapping? Totally. And then, of course, I began to entertain those nagging voices that swirl around in our heads in times like this. "You're ugly. You're not good enough. You can't do anything right." And what's even worse, I began to whisper these ugly words as *truth* in my heart. Sound familiar?

Ladies, why do we do this? There is absolutely zero truth in any of those words.

Psalm 139 says that God planned and created each of us. We are fearfully and wonderfully made—*fearfully* meaning "with great awe." Ecclesiastes 3:11 states that God made *everything* beautiful in its time. That means me. That means you. When we choose to love and serve God, we become radiant with that God-beauty and naturally share it with everyone around us.

Beloved of God, let these truths wash over you. Believe them and implant them deep within your heart. Don't let those negative voices have their way with you. Kick them to the curb and be radiant with the phenomenal glow that is forever within you. No matter what colossal *faux pas* you make, it will never negate this awe-inspiring beauty God created in you.

Dear God, I so much want to own this radiant beauty spoken of here. Please help me feel it and believe it. Help me remember and apply your words of affirmation to my heart and kick those negative voices to the curb. Help me walk in your love as I joyfully serve you.

Klutz to Conqueror

by Becki James

Let us strip off every weight that slows us down, especially the sin that so easily trips us up. And let us run with endurance the race God has set before us. We do this by keeping our eyes on Jesus, the champion who initiates and perfects our faith.

HEBREWS 12:1–2 (NLT)

TEENAGERS DO STUPID things. I was a teenager once. Once was enough. In twelfth grade, we decided to meet for breakfast and posted details for others on the chalkboard. My glory days immortalized the day my name was etched in white: "Becki Watson: Klutz of the Week Award!"

That wintry morning, we packed into Amy's Volkswagen Beetle, an orange, wind-up wonder. Juddering, it reeled and let loose like a coiled toy. Off we went, shoulder to shoulder, elbows jabbing ribs, with glacial vinyl seats impairing circulation. Nevertheless, merriment chattered through teeth and blue lips. Wedged against the window, with my free hand swaying overhead, I clutched the one-bolted, leather life-loop that represented safety.

We swayed the curve to a red light, allowing the merging traffic their moment in green glory. But, with nothing glorious appearing, that beacon thawed the cerebral flow for someone who bellowed, "red light fire drill!" And with that, a topple of girls broke past leather loops to beat that light by circling the Beetle. Roaring like Polar Plunge warriors, our bare hands clawed the creamsicled hood as tennies slid wildly. Ahead of me, victory shouts hailed. My final strides, however, faltered from the overpowering rumble that barreled around the bend.

Whoosh!

Whack!

I hit the road just as the passing thirty-ton snowplow forced my hair skyward.

Mouth gaping, I dove headlong into the car. Unscathed, but a klutz, nonetheless.

Sometimes, laughing at myself helps me embrace change. I struggle with distraction. Days pass before I realize I tripped. Bunny trails that seem valid consume my focus. As God's child, my focus belongs to him. When I take my eyes off him, I lose his direction, his purpose, and the joy of his presence.

God's remedy for my clumsy performance is Jesus. His forgiveness strips the weight of sin, allowing me to run well. My insufficient strength causes me to stumble. But he is present, extending his hand to help me. My race is a gift to help me understand his love.

Living in his presence means I continually refocus on his purpose. The best lifeline is to tether myself to his throne with prayer. It provides unlimited strength and unending love. Living in his presence means focusing on Jesus.

Abba Father, I come before your throne. Thank you for your patience and presence. Help me to focus on you by tethering myself to you in prayer.

Put a Fermata on Grace

by Robin J. Steinweg

<hr/>

*For from his fullness we have all
received, grace upon grace.*

JOHN 1:16 (ESV)

"OK, CHOIR," I said. "Take your pencils. Put a fermata on grace."

"What did she say?" A soprano hadn't heard.

A bass responded, "Hold on to grace."

The altos needed to be heard as well. "Hold on to grace longer."

"How do you make a fermata?"

"Just write *hold it longer* on grace."

A lone tenor piped up, "I lost my pencil. Can I borrow yours? What word was it we're supposed to hold—grace?"

I don't always hear the interchanges between choir members (sometimes it's better that way!). But I'm grateful this one didn't escape me.

Put a fermata on grace. In our choir piece, that meant to insert a bird's-eye-like symbol above the note falling on the word *grace.* The fermata tells the musician to linger there longer than usual. The comments of the choir members highlighted to me a whole lot more than the need to remain on a particular note.

I could apply the term to life. Jesus's story about the servant who owed an impossible amount of money comes to mind.

The king decided to enslave him until the debt was paid. But the man pleaded, and the king showed grace to him by completely forgiving his debt. The man left with joy. But then he demanded payment from someone who owed him a much smaller amount of money. When that person couldn't pay and begged for mercy, the lender had him arrested and put in prison. Though the servant had been forgiven an unpayable debt, he did not offer grace to another.

If I linger over anything, let it be grace—Christ's forgiveness, though I don't deserve it. Let me pitch a tent there. Let me offer it to others. I'll *accelerando* over grudges. I'll put a pause before angry reactions. I'll place measures of rest over harried times. But above all, I determine to do one thing from now on: hold on to grace.

To embellish life with beauty, add grace notes.

The Family That Camps Together

by Robin Steinweg

Because the foolishness of God is
wiser than men.

1 Corinthians 1:25 (nkjv)

*I*S IT POSSIBLE these days to raise a happy, well-adjusted family? When our boys were little, we listened faithfully to Dr. James Dobson's *Focus on the Family* program. We learned a great deal and developed confidence in the advice we heard. One day, he mentioned a poll taken of successful Christian families. Something they all had in common—camping.

Without hesitation, we scoured garage sales and thrift stores for equipment. We borrowed how-to books from the library and collected recipes for campfire meals. We found an available site at a state park and loaded the car till the bumper scraped the driveway.

My husband had never camped in his life. I had fond memories of camping as a young child. The rain, the long, soggy treks to the outhouse, the lake leeches attached to my screaming sister's legs, the mosquitoes carrying me off. How could I describe such delights to my uninitiated family? I didn't. They could experience it for themselves.

The book of Proverbs tells us wisdom will protect us. Wisdom is supreme—so get it, if it costs all you have. Wisdom might come through God's Word, or sometimes he plants it within us. But then there are the times he allows us to walk all on our own through an experience so we can develop our wisdom muscle.

I should have seen it coming. A husband who dislikes the unexpected. A son who believed he had a future in entomology (the study of bugs). A toddler who believed every insect was a death-bearing scorpion, every body of water full of stinging jellyfish. And me, with allergy-induced asthma. A thin sheet of canvas wasn't a proper filter from ragweed that spread pollen like guests showering rice on newlyweds. Nor did it filter the whoops of drunken neighbors starting their weekend early.

By the time we folded up our sodden tent (of course, it rained), we were only on speaking terms with our sons. We got over it eventually and learned some valuable lessons. It's wonderful that programs like *Focus on the Family* teach successful parenting skills, but it's a good idea to check with God before jumping into things. What works for other families may not be God's best for yours.

Yes, it's possible to raise a happy, well-adjusted family these days. But leave camping for campers!

The family that camps together may end up soaked and ornery.

Lessons from a Dog

by Sandy Lipsky

*The sheep that are My own hear and are
listening to My voice; and I know them,
and they follow Me.*

JOHN 10:27 (AMPC)

*P*ANDA IS A dog. My husband would say she is my dog because wherever I go, she follows. If I sit down to write, she lays on a rug in my office. When I use the restroom, Panda sleeps outside the door. I'm on the move throughout the day and rarely pause in one place for long. Up and down are Panda's movements as she trails me.

It's easy to see how an observer would accuse her of laziness and attribute her behavior to lethargy. Walk, sleep, wait, watch, and sleep again. My perspective toward Panda's behavior recently changed after reading God's Word.

As I pondered John 10:27, I looked at the white, short-haired, beluga-like companion snoring at my feet. She appeared to be sleeping but inwardly was on high alert. As soon as I stood, her head popped up, and she watched for my next move. Her eyes followed to see where I was heading. When I went out of view, she stood to draggle behind me.

Daily, when I call her name, she comes. In between commands, she waits. Her obedience is steadfast. As soon as she hears my voice, she is at my feet. "What do you need?" her eyes ask.

She desires to make me happy.

Does God want me to be like Panda?

The scriptures say: be still, be watchful, follow him, listen for his voice, and desire to please him. All these are attributes I see in Panda.

"What do you do all day?" is a question Panda and I have fielded in the past. The query causes a bristling in my spirit but has the opposite effect on Panda. She wags her tail and answers with a look that simply says, "Wait for my master."

I want to be like Panda. I want to be patient and watchful. Listening for my master, I want to be ready when he calls.

Father, give me discernment to distinguish your voice from the clamoring ones of the world. Help me patiently wait for your instructions and follow where you lead.

A Giggle a Day Keeps the Grumpy Away

by Michelle Rayburn

*So I concluded there is nothing better than to be
happy and enjoy ourselves as long as we can.*

ECCLESIASTES 3:12 (NLT)

I GLANCED UP FROM my laptop to see his grubby hands
held to the french door of my home office. Despite who-
knows-what clasped within those hands, it was the twinkle in his
eyes and his silly grin that tickled my curiosity. *What in the world?*
He pressed his nose to the glass.

"Look what I brought you."

I hoped it was a brownie but knew better. As he unfurled his
fingers, the glossy face and bulging eyeballs of a plump frog stared
back at me from my husband's palm.

Yes. My husband.

"Take that back outside, please. Thank you. I don't need
office help today."

Practically skipping because he had managed to draw an
eyeroll from me, he walked his grass-covered shoes back up the
hallway. The screen door thumped, then I heard the lawnmower
start up again.

This sort of thing is common in our household. Somewhere inside of my fifty-something-year-old husband is the wonder and delight of an eight-year-old boy. He lives for fun and amusement. While his playfulness can be somewhat annoying when I'd prefer him to be serious, most of the time, his mischievous and rascally ways inspire me to experience more enjoyment in life.

Surely every family has at least one person who is more in tune with their good-humored side. It might be a beloved uncle, your kid sister, a parent, even you! Or your spouse. My husband provides a daily life-lesson for me about what it means to be happy and enjoy ourselves as long as we can. I'm quite sure God blessed me with him more than thirty years ago to prevent me from becoming a first-rate curmudgeon. God has put people like that in your life too.

How long has it been since you had a belly laugh? Take a few moments to lift your spirits, brighten your day, and find joy by calling or hanging out with your fun family member. Thank them for helping you enjoy yourself—because the Bible says it's good for you. Plus, your eyeroll and a giggle or two might make *their* day.

Father in heaven, thank you for putting people in my family who are filled with your delight and joy. I pray for opportunities to share a smile and a mutual blessing today.

Family

Bursting with Thanks

by Robin Steinweg

*Give thanks in all circumstances; for this is the
will of God in Christ Jesus for you.*

1 THESSALONIANS 5:18 (ESV)

I DECIDED ONE YEAR that my mom needed a break from cooking the whole Thanksgiving dinner. She and Dad determined they wanted everyone at their house. They would provide the big pull-out table and some side dishes, and traveling relatives could bring fresh fruit or relishes. It was my graduation from contributing Pillsbury crescent rolls and a can of Green Giant Niblets. I would roast (heavenly choir sings) *the turkey.*

In preparation, I watched PBS cooking shows and checked out cookbooks from the library. I even found a video for my husband on how to carve a turkey. Thus equipped, I felt confident. After all, I come from good Scandinavian cooking stock.

We ordered a turkey big enough to feed nearly twenty people. He barely fit in my oven. I took no chances. He came with a pop-out thermometer and gravy pouch, and I stuck him in one of those convenient cooking bags. I glanced over the directions, noting how much time he'd need to cook. After a newlywed fiasco in which I served my husband's bosses nearly raw chicken, I thought I'd err on the side of well done. I'd cook it a bit longer, but with a cover over the pan so no moisture would escape. The fragrance soon promised a mouth-watering meal.

Pressed for time at the end with all the foods needing to be finished at the same time, I whisked it all from the oven to a towel-lined box along with some pumpkin pies and potatoes supreme. I thought I would burst with pleasure at supplying the main dish for the first time.

Mom stood by to help lift the turkey out of the pan when we arrived. My husband stood by ready to carve. My older sister stood by, curious. The guests, seated, seemed to suspend their breathing as I raised the cover to reveal—a perfect wreck of a bare carcass. It looked like a bomb had landed in its middle. My husband would not need his carving lessons, with the turkey in bite-sized shreds. I'd forgotten to cut vent holes in the cooking bag.

Let's see. Humility? That's an important lesson. Plan ahead more? Be better prepared? Count it all joy when you face trials of many kinds? They say that at such times, a person's life passes before their eyes. But I took comfort as a verse from 1 Peter flashed to mind: "Love makes up for practically anything." Then I obeyed the next verse: "Be quick to give a meal to the hungry" (1 Peter 4:8–9 MSG).

Thank God if you belong to a family who loves you whether you succeed or fail. Even if they never let you live it down.

College Coping

by Robin Steinweg

*To everything there is a season, and a time for
every matter or purpose under heaven.*

Ecclesiastes 3:1 (ampc)

I ONCE HEARD SOMETHING Mark Twain said about raising
teens. He suggested they be put in a barrel and fed through a
hole. At sixteen, you close up the hole.

We never went through that. In fact, we can't get enough of
our sons. Nope, the trouble we had was Texas. The three-year Bible
college that fit for our oldest boy was in Dallas, a thousand miles
away. I don't hold Texans personally responsible for this.

There ought to be support groups for families with youngsters
going off into the world. It should begin with Lamaze—special
breathing exercises to get you through a prolonged transition.
Maybe ice chips. Or visualizing your young adult in your happy
place or right at the kitchen table.

Parenting classes should include at least one week of
preparing to say goodbye. Pain management clinics might at least
offer brochures on how to cope.

I turned to others who had (apparently) lived through it. This
was not helpful. Some teared up, put a comforting (?) hand on my

arm, and could say nothing. Others were obviously in denial. They said they'd hardly been able to wait for the "blessed event."

His senior year included the last Christmas concert, last fundraiser, last choir tour, and last prom. Summer brought his last week of working at the local grocer's, last family fun day at Wisconsin Dells, last worship service together. I remembered all the "firsts" we'd had with him: the first goodbye as he left the womb, first smile, first tooth, first time he sat up, first word, first steps, first haircut.

We squeezed his belongings into the car. It seemed as if I were helping to build my own gallows. I can't believe we took him down there—and left him. But we did it. We drew closer to the Lord, he helped us survive, and finally, the three years ended.

Now on the other side of college, I encourage parents who are facing this separation. God is faithful to guard and keep our children even when they're far from home. If I were to add my own observations to the third chapter of Ecclesiastes, I'd say there's a time to raise our children, a time to hold them close, a time to release them, and sometimes . . . a time to welcome them back!

Here's to many happy future homecomings.

Find reasons to rejoice in all the first, lasts, and in-betweens. Trust in the First and Last, who gives more grace than sufficient to meet every need.

The Thanksgiving That (Almost) Wasn't

by Edna Earney

———•◉•———

For this is the love of God, that we
keep his commandments. And his
commandments are not burdensome.

1 JOHN 5:3 (ESV)

I HAVE ONE KID in bed with a temperature, a surly pre-teen sulking because her friends are out of town, and my husband is working his second job after finishing the midnight shift as a police officer. My toddler starts crying in her bedroom because her sister won't play with her.

I realize I forgot three things at the grocery store last night. And it's noon—on Thanksgiving—I haven't cooked anything but the pumpkin pie.

Overwhelmed. Short-fused.

Inadequate. A failure.

"Mommy, why are you crying? It's okay, Mommy. It's okay."

My sweet little girl has no idea why I am so upset. She doesn't feel any pressure to maintain family traditions on this holiday. Wait a minute. Do my girls even care whether we have roast turkey today? Or homemade cornbread dressing? They probably care about having whipped cream on their pie. But I forgot to buy the whipped cream.

God, I could use some direction here. "My commandments are not burdensome." *That sounds good. Anything else?*

The phone rings. "Hello. Oh, hi! You want to come over? Today? No, no plans. Yes, just us. Okay, see you soon."

Really? Visitors now? I should at least start a pot of coffee.

I slip into the middle bedroom to talk with my sick one. "Honey, guess who just called. Mr. and Mrs. Floyd, your Sunday school teachers. They are coming over this afternoon to pray for you to get well."

An hour later, the Floyds ring the doorbell. They pray for our daughter. They have brought decorated cookies to share. And they wave away my constant apologies for not being the hostess I think I should be. When I tear up about my Thanksgiving dinner that looks pretty hopeless, they commiserate but point out that I can still be a good mom and have a fun holiday with my girls—even without turkey and stuffing. They tell stories of holidays gone wrong with their grown boys, and we laugh. I feel better.

God has given us many wonderful traditions to keep. We partake of communion, gather with other believers, and tell our children of God's love and deliverance. But he never commanded that we cook a huge meal on Thanksgiving, especially at the expense of harmony in our home.

The chicken nuggets and french fries that day weren't fancy, but they were fine. We colored pictures of Pilgrims and turkeys while dinner baked. And we thanked God for the food, our family, and caring friends.

Dear God, my protector and provider, thank you for my family, my friendships, and especially for those friends who help me re-center my perspective and priorities.

The Empty Car

by Mary Harker

And these words that I command you today shall be on your heart. You shall teach them diligently to your children, and shall talk of them when you sit in your house, and when you walk by the way, and when you lie down, and when you rise.

DEUTERONOMY 6:6–7 (ESV)

AN EMPTY CAR sits in our driveway, like a butterfly's deserted chrysalis. There is noticeable rust. The leaky sunroof is fixed with duct tape. It rests forlorn and isolated, yet, it is a picture of precious treasures passed on to our son.

The car represents the warm cocoon in which he was nurtured and loved, where he took the first steps and spoke his first words. I nostalgically think back on the first day of Pre-K 4. Drew burst into the room, confident to tackle his new world—I shed quiet tears in the parking lot. School subjects challenged him, but we were well-pleased when he graduated from high school with honors. Under our roof, he learned the importance of loving God and others. We taught and he mastered necessary life skills.

Time spent in the car developed our relationship. We talked, cried, and laughed together, sharing our hearts. He grew from car seat to driver seat. Like the butterfly, my son broke out of the chrysalis and took off into the world. The vacated vehicle remains behind, a reminder of bygone years.

My husband and I aimed to launch our son into the world, rooted in God, to impact his world for Christ. Recently, he sent me a text and included a song based on the hymn, "Great Is Thy Faithfulness," saying it reminded him of me. I sang this hymn over him every night as I put him to bed when he was young. It was a testimony of God's faithfulness in our lives. My heart filled with joy, and tears flowed as I saw how God answered our prayers. God's truth appeared embedded in his heart.

Whatever your season of parenting, take heart. Whether you are walking a crying newborn during the midnight hours or trailing after an energetic toddler, your efforts are not in vain. Perhaps you are driving to extracurricular activities or helping your struggling student with homework. Take time to pray together during the successes and the challenges. Maybe you are praying and waiting for the daughter making poor choices or the prodigal who has lost his way. Remember the mercy and grace of God and pass it on, like a rich inheritance, to your child. Dear parent, God blessed you with offspring. Be strong and courageous, fulfilling the mission he gave you.

Father, thank you for the precious gift of children. As I study your Word, help me pass your truths to the next generation. I pray your hand will be on my child today.

Their Favorite Word

by Mary E. Curcio

I do not set aside the grace of God.

GALATIANS 2:21 (NKJV)

I WAS A CHILD with parental responsibilities. As the oldest of seven siblings, daily, I was responsible for their care. That meant cooking meals, doing laundry, making sure they did their homework, and disciplining them. A lot of responsibility for a child who never had the opportunity to be a child.

I believed parents—and parental siblings—are supposed to be perfect, so I wanted everything around me to be just so. Throughout my school years, I had to get perfect grades, be the best student, and always be right. Then I became a parent of my own children.

Often, my children asked my mom to tell them a story about how I was bad. They were trying to get some dirt on me. My mom replied, "Not my Mary. She was always a good girl." I reveled in those words.

At church one Sunday, our pastor's sermon was on grace. He shared from the Bible how God and Jesus displayed grace. When we got home, I discovered my children had done something they knew not to. When I proceeded to discipline them, they said, "Mom, didn't you hear the sermon today?"

I said, "Of course." They asked for grace and reminded me that God gave his children grace.

I thought about giving them grace but couldn't. My expectations of good behavior would not allow me. For years, I taught them godly principles. They knew the rules and received my desired discipline.

I once thought grace and discipline together was an oxymoron. I soon realized that my expectation of perfection from my children was overbearing. Because I wanted to be perfect, I expected them to be good all the time. Sadly, I believed my image as a perfect parent came from my children being good. If they weren't perfect, then I wasn't the best parent I wanted to be.

God is so good to teach truth. My reputation as a parent doesn't depend on my children's behavior. If I believed that God gave consequences based on my behavior, then I would never receive grace. I resolved to change the way I disciplined and prayed earnestly for wisdom. As I sought the scriptures, the Holy Spirit taught me when to discipline and when to give grace. And if I couldn't discern when to give grace, I chose to err on the side of grace. If I was wrong, I trusted God to take care of it.

This new grace-discipline process is a good model of how God gives grace. In discipline, you can display grace. When you can't exempt your children from discipline, your discipline can be gracious. When you struggle to know when to give grace or discipline, ask God for grace. Your children will love you *and* God for it.

Father, thank you that you don't expect me to be perfect.
Thank you for continually being gracious to me.

Bonfire Reflections

by TLC Nielsen

"Fear not, for I have redeemed you; I have called you by name, you are mine. When you pass through the waters, I will be with you . . . when you walk through fire you shall not be burned, and the flame shall not consume you."

ISAIAH 43:1–2 (ESV)

*I*N MY FAMILY, I am the fire starter. "Time for s'mores," my children would say, and outside I'd go to gather enough twigs and tree limbs to start a fire. You didn't have to ask me twice, childhood camper that I'd been. As a kid, we used to spend weeks living at campgrounds closest to the university from which my parents took classes. So, I learned how to make the best fires: grab a few pages of newspaper, add some smaller twigs tepee-style, and top it with thick branches. I continued the skill as a parent— creating memories. Now that my kids are grown and on their own, I miss those days of making bonfires and toasting marshmallows together.

In the uncertainty of a crazy year, my better half and I redis-covered this family tradition amid the unrelenting stress—the joy of a bonfire as dusk settles in. The powerful winds of the chang-ing seasons provided far too many fallen branches. To burn up this abundance of wood, the two of us have cooked over the fire, warmed our feet with its heat, and found companionship around the flames. Roasting meat and cooking flatbread over the fire pit widened our outdoor menu, but the perfectly toasted marshmallow remains a staple, especially when the kids visit.

My favorite part of the bonfire, however, is grappling with the day's adventures until we lapse into silence and stare into the embers. It's in the dim glow that God often speaks, pointing out his design from tree to ashes, which enrich the soil and provide new growth. God's Spirit warms us in the chill of the night, helping me see his hand in the hard circumstances we face. He assures me that it's from the ashes of these tough times that new things can grow, especially for those he has called by name.

This is what God expects us to do with the windswept debris of life—gather it, pile it before him, and trust that he can transform it as kindling into something better.

Lord Jesus, thank you for making something new out of the tough things in life. Teach me to trust you through it all. Please bond each one of us in the family together with your presence.

Planning Ahead for Love

by Lori Lipsky

Love one another with brotherly affection.
Outdo one another in showing honor.

ROMANS 12:10 (ESV)

MY MOM EXCELLED at celebrating her children's birthdays. Even if we didn't get expensive gifts, she made the day special by allowing us to skip making our beds for the day. We'd get to choose our favorite food for dinner and select what type of cake she'd make for us. There would be candles to blow out, and we sang the "Happy Birthday" song.

Her extra investment of time showed us love. Now that I'm older, I recognize her sacrifice. She made our beds, shopped for groceries to cook our favorite meal, and baked a cake. Always, we received a gift or two. She'd taken the time to shop and wrap the gifts, too. Through her sacrifice, she made us feel special. She showed us she loved us.

I celebrated another birthday not long ago—one of those significant ones. My milestone age ends with zero again. Maybe I should be old enough to say I don't care about my birthday anymore, but I do. My mother is no longer here to show love to me on my special day, but my sister, Sandy, is around.

Long before my birthday this year, Sandy purchased a plane ticket. She lives 860 miles away. She took the time to ship my gifts to our dad's house. She asked me months earlier about cakes. I remembered a chocolate cake with white frosting my mother made a number of times. My sister searched for Mom's recipe and took the extra trouble to make the delicious cake using gluten-free flour since I'm gluten sensitive.

On my birthday, my dad and sister came to my house and spent the entire day. We ate lunch and played a few of my favorite games together. When my husband got home from work, we ordered dinner from a nearby restaurant. After he went to pick it up, we gathered around the table for our delicious meal. My husband, my children, my granddaughter, and my dad were there, but it was my sister who sacrificed a large block of time to fly up and make everything happen.

The cake she baked brought back wonderful childhood memories. There were gifts to unwrap, too. They showed me love in ways too numerous to count on that one day.

The Bible tells us we ought to love one another. Love can be shared through time spent, gifts given, signs of affection, and through thoughtful words. Who might I show love to today? How will I choose to do it?

*Lord, help me to love others. Love comes
from you. Show me the way.*

A Walk Toward Wisdom

by Lori Lipsky

*Teach us to number our days that we may
get a heart of wisdom.*

PSALM 90:12 (ESV)

HAVE YOU EVER asked the Lord for wisdom? A sermon on the topic of wise living made a strong impression on me, even though the assistant pastor gave the message twenty years ago. My daughters were about eight and eleven years old at the time. The pastor challenged us to walk around a cemetery and think about the brevity of life. He encouraged us to do it before the following Sunday, if possible.

At the time, I was no stranger to cemeteries. Because of my interest in family genealogy, I'd searched cemeteries for headstones of relatives. While growing up, my parents tolerated my interest and drove out of their way to help me find family gravestones in nearby states.

After I married and our daughters came along, our family took several trips to visit burial sites of former U.S. presidents and founding fathers. We homeschooled, and it was a way of combining my interest in presidents with history lessons for the children.

Even though my girls had visited cemeteries, we'd never done it to consider the brevity of life. Most of us don't like to discuss death with our children. It isn't part of our everyday conversation.

The Bible reminds us that we don't know what tomorrow will bring. After all, the mortality rate is close to 100 percent. Psalm 90 says understanding that we don't live forever can lead to wisdom. Wisdom is something we all want for ourselves and our children.

The day after the pastor's challenge, I took my girls to the largest cemetery in the area. On our way, we picked up cemetery flowers. Hoping to teach my daughters respect, we looked for graves of veterans and placed the flowers there. We stopped at many headstones and learned what we could about the people who had once lived but were now laid to rest. When we returned home we did more research. It was eye-opening.

The Bible says we are like grass. We will eventually wilt and die. In the meantime, we've been given a life to live. If we remember to number our days, it might help us to live more wisely.

Lord, I'm thankful for my life. You've said in your Word that my days on earth are numbered. Please help me to make wise choices with the time you grant.

Meals in the Freezer

by Lori Lipsky

*Go to the ant, O sluggard; consider her ways, and be wise.
Without having any chief, officer, or ruler, she prepares her
bread in summer and gathers her food in harvest.*

PROVERBS 6:6–8 (ESV)

M Y ANCESTORS LEARNED the benefits of storing the harvest of gardens and fields for the winter to come. It's a natural part of farm life. During my childhood years, we lived in town, but my dad gardened. My mother cooked and served us the yields of the earth. She froze or canned the rest so our family could enjoy produce from the garden all year round.

I've always lived in town, but my family roots are planted in farmland. Rich, Iowan farmland. Each of my parents and grandparents spent at least a portion of their childhood on a farm, where they learned lessons of hard work and diligence.

I've witnessed both my mother and my next-door neighbor cook and freeze in times of plenty in order to prepare for winter. There's wisdom in planning ahead and being prepared.

Beyond my childhood years, and even when she was in her eighties, my mom continued to cook and freeze meals in times of abundance. Since they lived in town, she'd look for sales at her local grocery store. If ground chuck was on sale, she'd buy in bulk and freeze quantities of chili and spaghetti sauce. If she served ham for dinner, she might cook a big pot of bean soup to use the left-over ham.

When a minor medical procedure led to a serious infection, my mother was in the hospital for over two months. My dad spent time with her every day, but in the evenings, he could return home and still heat and enjoy my mother's delicious cooking if he remembered to remove a meal container from the freezer that morning. Even after her death, he benefited from many meals she'd stored up earlier in the season.

After sixty-five years of living with my mother and eating her wonderful cooking, the blessing of those meals she'd stocked in the freezer can't be overstated. By the time the freezer emptied, my dad was emotionally ready to cook for himself.

Heavenly Father, I ask for wisdom and diligence.
Help me to learn as I study the ant.

A Quest for Beauty

by Lori Lipsky

*One thing I have desired of the L*ORD*, That will
I seek: That I may dwell in the house of the L*ORD
*All the days of my life, To behold the beauty of the L*ORD*.*

PSALM 27:4 (NKJV)

I DIDN'T REALIZE IT as I was growing up, but my parents
collected art. We didn't take family vacations because they
were too expensive. We rarely ate out, and we never had a new car.
But my parents invested in art.

Now and then, they'd buy an original painting from a local
artist at a weekend art show. Once or twice a year, crafters and
artists rented space at a local mall for a weekend. People from the
small towns in the area came and investigated. My folks were there
among the browsers. Sometimes they saved enough to buy a painting or a print.

Mom loved beautiful ceramic, china, and crystal collectibles.
For Mother's Days, birthdays, and Christmases she'd usually
receive at least one pretty item to add to her collection.

A few years ago, I asked my parents about the paintings
and prints hung in their home. They remembered where they'd
purchased each piece, and they shared what they knew about the
artists. I asked why they chose to spend money on art and beautiful

things. Dad said they thought art was important, and they enjoyed looking at the items they'd chosen. Mom added that they liked to support artists, and she enjoyed pretty things. It's natural to be attracted to beautiful things and beautiful people.

We don't all agree about what art is and what looks beautiful. Different art appeals to different people. My favorite color is blue. Yours may be green. And since we all change as we age, our opinion of what or who is beautiful may change, also.

The creator of the white tiger, the Mandarin fish, and the scarlet macaw knows all about beauty. He's the maker of the most beautiful lake in the world, and the most gorgeous waterfall. The most creative landscape artist of all time painted into being the loveliest beaches and rivers.

All true beauty has its root in the Creator of the world. He creates beauty and all good things. But there's more. The Bible tells us the Lord himself is beautiful. Scripture says to invest our time and energy seeking him and gazing on his beauty.

Lord, you are the supreme artist of the universe. Thank you for the beauty you've created here on earth. Remind me to look to the heavens and seek your beauty.

Lord, Help Us!

by Gina Stinson

—◦●◦—

And you shall teach them to your children, speaking of
them when you sit in your house and when you walk
along the road, when you lie down and when you rise up.

DEUTERONOMY 11:19 (AMPC)

MOMS MATTER. FOR all those days where you find yourself wondering if what you do really makes a difference,
consider this your personal pat on the back, and be assured, it
does. From diaper changing to carpooling to bedtime stories, you
are making memories and shaping the lives of future leaders. What
you do most definitely matters.

Whether we consider ourselves good or bad moms, the influence we have on the lives God entrusts to us is immeasurable. In
fact, it's a little frightening. The words I speak over my children on
a daily basis help form their own thoughts about the world, God,
their self-worth, their family, and more. Let's face it, my parenting
skills—good or bad—are going to be mirrored in my kids. *Lord,*
help us.

In a world that screams out to kids about their weight, their
athletic ability, and their grade-point average, I'm instructed to
scream (in a good way) about the love of God, how valuable they

are in God's eyes, while at the same time instilling a biblical world-view, a love for others, and how to be a decent human being. It's a daunting task. Somebody's gotta do it. Someone will.

Good parenting isn't for the lazy. If I won't parent my kids, the world will do it for me. God's Word tells me I am to instill God-things in my children from sunup to sundown. I have so much to do and so little time. Eighteen to twenty-two years hardly seems like enough time to get it all in. Thankfully, God is on my side. He is my help and guide; he shows me opportunities to help my children through life. Christian parents don't walk alone. With our guidebook—the Bible—and the Holy Spirit, we can make a difference in this generation. *Lord, please help us.*

Lord, thank you for the children you have given me. My heart desires to train them up as you have instructed in your Word. Give me wisdom and discernment to know what to do and grace for the days when I fall short. Give me strength to stay focused on this precious task before me.

What I Learned from Jesus and Jennifer

by Edna Earney

*Don't jump to conclusions—there may be a
perfectly good explanation for what you just saw.*

PROVERBS 25:8 (MSG)

IN A RECENT Facebook post, my daughter Jennifer told about a conversation with her six-year-old son:

> **Jennifer:** Did you just roll your eyes at me?
>
> **Son:** Mommm, [tearing up] I didn't mean for you to actually SEE me roll my eyes. I mean, I didn't mean for you to LOOK at me and it LOOK LIKE I was rolling my eyes.
>
> **Jennifer:** Sooooo that's a yes, then?

Of course, I chuckled as I read the post. My grandson is a sensitive soul. He does not like for his mom to be upset with him. His quick recovery, that he only *looked like* he was rolling his eyes, tickled my charm button.

A good friend added a smiley face and commented, "Why do moms ask questions they already know the answer to? Used to kill me when my mom did that."

Jennifer replied that she often asks a question, especially if she thinks she knows the answer. As I read her reply to my friend, I saw God working in this young momma. "I don't want to assume his intent," she said. "Sometimes I interpret one intent, only to find out he meant something different. Instead of hurting his feelings, I move to a teachable moment. Also, I ask to make him take a second to rethink his actions. Asking a question can lead to his realizing what I thought and open up a conversation. Simply saying, 'Don't roll your eyes at me,' is accusatory and goes in one ear and out the other. That few seconds while asking gives me time to gather my next words and take a calming breath (or two) in order to better address the situation. There is a method to my madness :-)."

Similarly, Jesus asked questions and made requests. He transformed people by making them think. Granted, it would be nice to have his divine insight! But consider these:

- He asked the invalid at the pool in Bethesda, "Do you want to get well?" (John 5:6 MSG). That seems to have an obvious answer, doesn't it?

- He asked the rich young ruler, "Why do you call me good? No one is good except God alone" (Luke 18:19 ESV). Jesus points out to the ruler no one can be called *good*, not even the ruler who had followed all the rules of the Jewish religion.

- He asked the Samaritan woman at the well for a drink of water. This request gave him time to converse with her, leading to her salvation (John 4:7).

I need to remember to ask more questions, just like Jesus and Jennifer.

Oh, God, remind me daily that you are the ultimate judge and will rule over the only judgment that counts. Help me to take a breath and ask another question when I would rather jump to a conclusion.

Thought Bubbles in the Bathtub

by Edna Earney

———•◉•———

Likewise the Spirit helps us in our weakness. For we do not know what to pray for as we ought, but the Spirit himself intercedes for us with groanings too deep for words.

ROMANS 8:26 (ESV)

"*G*OD, I'M DONE. I don't know how to fix this mess," I cried, groaning and praying only a few simple words.

I had retreated to the bathtub, the only space in the house where I could be alone. I filled the tub with steamy water and rose-scented bubble bath. Still shaking from the arguments at dinner, I sank up to my nose. Our three teenage daughters had driven me to seek solitude and find solace in God.

I emptied out my hurt and confusion through cascading tears, then let my muscles relax into the warmth. That invisible but palpable embrace from God continued as he spoke in his still, quiet voice, uploading advice for my benefit. I wished for pen and paper—I needed to remember this! But in God's way, the instructions were simple, easy to remember, and made so much sense.

Confusion reigned several days of the week with my family's busy schedules. God gave these specific instructions:

1. **You've lost intimacy.** Tuesday night is now family night. Games, togetherness, talks, anything that doesn't separate

family members from each other. An inviolable date on the calendar.

2. **Friday nights—whoever walks in the door first from school orders pizza.** One large pepperoni, one large Hawaiian. This allows the flute player and the drill team members a chance to eat before they run to pre-game activities. It also keeps the budget from blowing up with multiple fast-food orders.

3. **Sunday after church—plan ahead.** Either eat sandwiches at home or have a plan for where you will eat. Everyone orders water to drink because ordering soda breaks the budget.

4. **Again, you've lost intimacy.** When one of the girls is grounded, that means she spends the day or night doing what you are doing. All day with her at your side will give you the opportunity to speak love and support into her life.

I climbed out of the tub, dressed, and called a family meeting. I shared those four points with my husband and our three girls. They received the ideas with just a few of their own groans. Was it my calm voice? God's preparation of their hearts? God's authoring of the plan? Probably that and more.

I have no recollection of how long we followed these guidelines. But I do know that my family was reassured that our God is a God of order, not chaos. Peace, not strife. Intimacy, not division.

*Our master planner, Alpha and Omega, thank you
for hearing my groanings and being compassionate
when I feel I have no way out of the pit. Thank you for
directing my steps as I seek to serve you.*

How Do You Know?

by Darla S. Grieco

*But the Helper, the Holy Spirit, whom the Father will
send in my name, he will teach you all things and
bring to your remembrance all that I have said to you.*

JOHN 14:26 (ESV)

AS I SAT typing on my laptop, I felt the stare of my precocious eight-year-old son fixated on me as my fingers
flitted across the keyboard.

"Can I help you?" I asked.

"How do you do that, Mom?" His face contorted.

"Do what?"

"How do you know what you're doin'? You aren't even lookin'
at the keyboard, and your fingers are going *really* fast."

"I don't know," I said, "I have a thought in my brain, and it
travels through my fingers. I guess that's the advantage of learning
how to type properly at a young age."

He rested his chubby cheeks on his hands as he considered
what I'd said.

Assuming our Q&A had finished, I returned to my typing.

"Mom."

I closed my laptop and joined my son on our front porch
stoop. "Yes, dear."

"Do you know when you mess up?"

I laughed. "Actually, I do. My brain realizes it almost immediately when I hit the wrong key. Then I stop to correct it. Sometimes I catch it quicker than others. But, yes, I am aware."

Our little talk reminded me of my journey as a Christian.

At first, when I turned my life over to Christ, I learned all I could through participating in Bible studies and learning from mentors. I applied one principle, then another. As time passed, I gained a deeper understanding of God's expectations for me.

I found that the more time I invested in learning his Word, praying, and spending time with him, the deeper my relationship with him grew. And as I allowed the Holy Spirit to do a work in my heart, I recognized more quickly when I made "a typo."

A lot like typing—the more we practice, the better we get.

I'm grateful for the ever-present Helper God has sent to signal me when I go astray. Of course, I'm ultimately responsible for how I respond—by hitting backspace and correcting it right away or re-examining the situation at a later time—but he always continues to teach and remind me how to walk in his ways.

Lord, help me to remain aware of your presence in my life. May I always heed your warnings and learn that which your Spirit has for me.

A Blemish in Jesus's Lineage

by Mary Harker

God decided in advance to adopt us into his own family
by bringing us to himself through Jesus Christ. This is
what he wanted to do, and it gave him great pleasure.

EPHESIANS 1:5 (NLT)

IMAGINE LOOKING INTO your genealogy and finding something unexpected. Like George W. Bush uncovering he's related to Hugh Hefner or Kate Middleton discovering she's connected to George Washington. This was considered scandalous news—not something they wanted the world to know. Similarly, Jesus has blemishes in his lineage, but he showed the whole world through Scripture. Take Rahab, the presumed prostitute, for example.

I can relate to Rahab, feeling unacceptable to be in Jesus's lineage. I have looked for love in all the wrong places. Given my heart too easily to someone to whom it should have never belonged. I hold on to attitudes that tear my spirit in two and harden my heart. Believe the lie that I am broken and not worth Jesus's time or attention. That is a lie from the enemy of my soul. He wants to lie, steal, and kill my joy and separate me from my heavenly Father.

Like Rahab, I also found the one true God of Israel, who is God of the universe. He has taken the broken pieces of my life and created something new and beautiful. The Japanese have an art form called Kintsugi. They reassemble broken fragments of pottery with threads of gold. The end result is more lovely than before being broken. This is a beautiful picture of how Jesus repairs the devastation of my past with something more precious than gold. His blood transforms and makes beauty out of the damage.

Anticipating the spies' imminent return, Rahab tied a scarlet cord to the window. It was a sign of protection over the home and everyone in it. God spared her and her family because of her obedience and trust. He also redeemed her past and grafted her into Israel's family as a chosen descendant of Jesus.

God redeems our past, as he did for Rahab. If we believe the crimson blood of Jesus redeems our soul for eternity, we too are grafted into his family. We can be confident he has a future and a plan for our lives and will see it through to completion.

Walk in courage and strength, dear one, assured that Jesus does not hide the shady parts of his genealogy. He takes the past and replaces it with a glorious future.

Father, I thank you that you are a God of redemption. You are not ashamed of who I am, but you are glad to call me your child. Despite my past, you have a future and a plan for me. You take my past and give me a glorious future.

Incoming

by Becki James

Before daybreak the next morning, Jesus got up
and went out to an isolated place to pray.

MARK 1:35 (NLT)

ID YOU EVER watch a puppy chase his tail? Dogs chase anything. The summer I turned forty, I ranked a five-star veteran in the M.O.M. Corps—Mother of Many. Call it a midlife crisis, but even in a platoon of humans, something lacked— something canine. I mean, kids are great, but puppies—puppies are pure cuteness! Using the big 4-0 as leverage, I assembled my troop and headed south, gaining possession of my lop-eared Boxer buddy. One look from those brown eyes, and I became the proud owner of a slobber-mouthed smoocher. Sawyer had plenty of wiggle, even if his only waggle came from a nub-tail. Chasing it, though, proved interesting. By the first snowfall, Sawyer discovered a new nemesis.

Snug in his bed, the pup awoke, stretching until his claws tapped the glass door. Scampering to attention, he cocked his muzzle at the snowy siege overtaking the backyard. Whimpering, he paced, eyes tracking the incoming enemy descending like paratroops. I slid the door open, and he sprang out with Boxer buoyancy.

Plop!

Feeling the frigid nip triggered his fight-or-flight. He yelped, retreating to the deck. Shaking his coat, he returned fire. Now he turned his attack on the air-strike. Up he leaped. Leap after leap, he chomped at the snowflakes. *Chomp!* Jowls flapped his face. *Jump! Chomp!*

Tears blurred my vision. I laughed until my sides ached.

Sometimes God speaks through comical situations. Sawyer enthusiastically fought the incoming snow. I'm like that. Dedicated to my family, I throttle forward as tasks pelt me from all sides. At times, I feel like I'm chasing my tail or chomping the air. I get knee-deep in the fluff before I realize I've been snowed. The kids need to be taxied. The dirty dishes stack up. There's a board meeting at ten. And no time for a shower—maybe later. All this as I grab an overlooked lunchbox while racing out the door. About three o'clock, I'm depleted, wanting take-out pizza.

While he ministered on earth, Jesus was busy. He loved, healed, taught, and beat back the enemy. People pressed him from all sides, demanding his human strength. Exhaustion could have prevailed, except he knew the counterbalance. He grounded himself in God's presence. Jesus rose before the commotion to find a solitary place to pray. When difficulties mounted, his focus remained stable.

Maybe mornings aren't your thing. Maybe solitude isn't realistic. That's okay. Wherever we are, God hears us. But Jesus taught us the importance of setting aside special time to talk with God. When we enter our Father's presence, we connect to our greatest source of strength and our greatest source of love. If I'm weary from chasing incoming cares, it's likely I need to pull back to his strength. I will be grounded in confidence if I walk with him.

Abba Father help me rely on the power of your presence.

Spiritual
Growth

The Hazards of the Hornworm

by Diana Leagh Matthews

━━━━━◦●◦━━━━━

*If we confess our sins, he is faithful and
just to forgive us our sins and to cleanse us
from all unrighteousness.*

1 John 1:9 (ESV)

*H*AVE YOU EVER been proud of an accomplishment, and then in what feels like a blink of an eye, it disappears? That happened to us recently at work.

"We'll have some big, juicy tomatoes next week." I stared down at the tomato plant that brimmed with cherry tomatoes. The eyes of the residents at the nursing home, where I work as activities director, widened with anticipation.

The following week, I passed by the tomato plant and noticed something looked wrong. At that moment, I did not have time to inspect it.

"Have you noticed the tomato plant? It's bare." My assistant approached me that afternoon. We walked into our outdoor courtyard and stared at the recently devoured plant.

"What happened?" We examined it, trying to understand how this could happen. Only three days ago, it abounded with life as if it were proud of its tomatoes that were ready to be plucked and eaten.

"My tomatoes?" One resident asked with tears in his eyes. He often checked the plant and was so disappointed.

With a little investigation, we discovered three tomato hornworms, a caterpillar-type insect, had consumed the plant into oblivion. Our research revealed how these animals quickly devour and destroy a once healthy plant.

This reminded me of how our sins, bad choices and negative actions, can worm their way into our lives, and like the tomato plant, our hearts become the home for destructive behavior and attitudes. We go about our day thinking everything is fine and dandy, but one small temptation leads to another and another until soon we have a problem with that area of our life. Before we know it, the transgression has become larger than we ever imagined, and we wonder how to get out of this infraction we've created.

Often, we think no one else will know about our disobedience, but then we carry it around without even realizing it. And even if no one else knows, we know. And God knows.

However, unlike our little tomato plant, we have hope. There is one who is willing and waiting to forgive us only if we ask.

Do you have a transgression you need to confess?

Heavenly Father, you know the sins I try to hide from everyone else, but they are never hidden from you. Forgive me of this sin and help me to walk in a manner that is honorable to you. We live in a hopeless world, but you have promised you are the light of the world, and when we come to you, we no longer walk in darkness. Thank you for loving me and forgiving me of my sins. Help me to be a shining beacon for you.

Taking Down the Leviathan

by Edna Earney

─────●◉●─────

*"Be strong and courageous. Do not fear or be in
dread of them, for it is the LORD your God who goes
with you. He will not leave you or forsake you."*

DEUTERONOMY 31:6 (ESV)

WE LOVE OUR little Shih Tzu doggies, Lizzie and
Dickens. They are cuddle bugs, but they transform
into crazed dynamos when the neighbor's ninety-pound Doberman
comes out to run his yard. You would think there were some kind
of signal that draws our furballs to zoom to the wooden fence,
jump three feet high, and bark as though they are ready to tear the
Doberman limb from limb. It's comical to watch—our dogs are
ten- to fifteen-pound lap dogs, and they "attack" an animal eight
times their size!

Doesn't that bring David and Goliath to mind? Or Moses
with Pharaoh? Joshua taking over the promised land? Maybe the
"monster in the closet" when we were little? I've had plenty of
those times when the job, the adversary next door, or even the
reluctant eighteen-year-old student seemed larger than life, beyond
my ability, and I needed to have my pup's perspective: *just get'em!*

A wise teaching colleague once consoled me with this advice:
"Eat a live frog first thing in the morning, and nothing worse will

happen to you the rest of the day." I looked up who originated this statement and see it is attributed to several people. Whoever said it, it's good advice! I've never eaten that live frog, but I've certainly faced that metaphorical Leviathan head-on at the beginning of the day, and I so often find that bite by bite, the monster isn't quite as big as I thought it was. (Leviathan is the name of a sea monster referenced in Scripture.)

Here are tips for taking down your Leviathan:

1. **Prayerfully make a list of steps.** The smaller the step, the better. Make these concrete steps to check off once completed. Do you have 150 thank-you notes to write from that last event? Your first step is to find the thank-you notes! Next step? Write two and address their envelopes.

2. **Look at the due date, if there is one.** Count the number of days between tomorrow and that due date. Divide the work, step by step, by the number of days.

3. **Understand that some will take longer than projected.** You might decide to break one of the steps you wrote down into several smaller steps. That's okay—just remember to adjust your timeline in number 2 above.

4. **Contact a trusted friend**. Explain your Leviathan and request that your friend pray for you as you complete your steps. Celebrate together as you make progress!

5. **Give God the glory when you see him show up!**

Lord, thank you for being with me as I face larger-than-life challenges. Help me to have the little dog's attitude as I face the big dogs!

Why Me?
Why *Not* Me?

by Mary E. Curcio

*And seek the peace of the city where I have caused you
to be carried away captive, and pray to the LORD for
it; for in its peace you will have peace.*

JEREMIAH 29:7 (NKJV)

MY HUSBAND AND I were nervous about moving to a new town where I would become the new school principal. We purchased a house and embarked on our new journey together.

As I settled into the school and community, I could see the Lord's hand in my new position. There were many Christians in the community and in my school. This encouraged me, but something didn't feel right. My spirit sensed something was amiss.

When I arrived home from work one day, I found a note on the table. My husband had left it for me. In a matter of seconds, everything I loved was gone. My twenty-five-year marriage, my home life, my identity as his wife, my security. I cried out to the Lord, "Why me?"

Dazed and grumbling, I couldn't accept what happened. Loneliness engulfed me. Every day I struggled to get out of bed. I was a stranger in a strange town. I called all my girlfriends, but none could console me except for one friend. I cried on the phone, "Why me?"

She said, "Why *not* you?"

I knew her words were from the Lord, but my heart refused to listen. Leaving this strange place would end my heartache. Home was where I would find peace, but I felt the Lord saying, "Stay." Escaping this place was my only peace, but I had no peace. I pleaded with the Lord to let me leave. That still small voice said, "Stay."

Stay was the same word Jeremiah told the Israelites. While the Israelites tended their sheep, the Babylonians captured them and took them back to Babylon to be their slaves. While in this strange land, they cried out to the Lord, "Why me?" They had no peace.

Jeremiah told the Israelites the Lord had allowed them to be taken captive. He instructed them to build houses, have families, plant gardens, and not murmur. They were to seek the peace of the city, for in its peace, they would have peace.

God's Word is timeless. If those words worked for the Israelites, they could work for me. I obeyed the Lord and planted a small garden. I prayed the Lord would bless my new home, my new friends, and community. I prayed for peace, and one by one God answered my prayers.

Lord, when I am fearful and lonely, I will call on your name and seek your Word first. It comforts me in my distress and teaches me to trust you.

Honor the King

by Mary E. Curcio

Honor all people. Love the brotherhood.
Fear God. Honor the king.

1 Peter 2:17 (NKJV)

I WAS AT THE end of my rope. Each time I pulled into the parking lot at work, I had an anxiety attack. Nothing I said or did improved my relationship with my superintendent. I had no idea how we had progressed to this point.

I moved to a new town and started a new career. Things normally come easy to me, but that first day on the job was overwhelming. The community, staff, and students seemed genuine and supportive, but I had much to learn.

My superintendent mentored me. Our relationship was very important to the community and district. Together we planned initiatives for each school and set those plans in motion. We were off to a good start.

I'm a to-do list girl. Finding a new church was my first priority. A house would be next. After a couple of church shopping Sundays, I settled in with my new church family. My new position and church made me happy.

My joy didn't last long. A new superintendent came. Unlike

my mentor, it was hard to communicate with my new boss. He was short-tempered and had outbursts of anger. Each time he entered my office, he berated or embarrassed me. My self-confidence dwindled, and my job performance suffered.

I didn't know anyone I could talk to, and my position required confidentiality. I was lonely and afraid and needed a confidante. At church one day, I broke down and cried to my pastor's wife. She had worked for this difficult superintendent. Her only words were, "Honor him."

It took some resolve, but I made up my mind to honor him. I gave my word to the Lord that no matter how bad things became, I would honor my boss. I found a verse I quoted daily. When things did not go well, I recited that verse. When others complained about him, I didn't. When my staff gossiped about him, I didn't.

Our relationship continued to decline. I begged the Lord to intervene, but nothing improved. I began to think God had abandoned me in my time of need.

At last, Christmas break came and went. On the first day back to work, I cringed as my superintendent entered my office. He said, "Mary, I just had the worst Christmas break ever. I have decided to bury the hatchet and mentor you to be the best administrator you can be."

And just like that, it was over. Over time, our relationship mended. I had tried in my own strength to fix it, but the Lord was the one who changed the situation. I learned that when I honored my boss, I honored God's Word and brought honor to God.

Lord, thank you that I can trust your Word to guide me through difficult trials. Thank you for rescuing me when I plead to you for deliverance.

In the Dark

by Stephenie Hovland

For God, who said, "Let light shine out of darkness," has shone in our hearts to give the light of the knowledge of the glory of God in the face of Jesus Christ.

2 Corinthians 4:6 (esv)

WHEN MY DAUGHTER was kindergarten age, we went to a mommy-daughter camp. One evening, we joined the other campers by the lake. We sat on hard wooden benches watching the setting sun's pink and orange rays reflected on the water. A bold bonfire blazed. Flames reached skyward as the sun settled into the earth. Our songs floated along in the cool night air.

When we finished our devotional time, the whole group started walking up the hill, through the woods. My daughter and I stopped to tie her shoelace and realized we had forgotten our flashlights. Before we knew it, we were behind the group just enough that we couldn't make out the path. We saw their flashlights bobbing ahead, but we couldn't see the ground and the tree roots right in front of us.

We stumbled along and held on to one another's hands. I said something about knowing the way, how we'd be there soon, and that there's nothing to worry about. (You know—the stuff you're supposed to say even though you don't feel it at all.) I started to panic, hoping I wouldn't fall and hurt myself or my daughter. The group had crested the hill, but we weren't out of the woods. It was dark—and a little scary.

Finally, we felt the path change from harsh roots to comforting grass. *Yes! We were safe again.* We trudged over the top of the hill and saw buildings, lamplights, and lots of happy, relaxed people.

It's funny how quickly we went from feeling safe and secure to lost and afraid. I find this happens in my everyday life too. I may study my Bible in the morning and hum a hymn, praying to God every day. But it doesn't seem to take much to start that little flicker of fear. If I'm not careful, fear rises and threatens to consume me.

Like our trek through the woods, I keep moving forward in my everyday life. I stumble a little and look for my light, Jesus. Life doesn't always feel as amazing as seeing a sun set on the lake next to a comfortable campfire. Life can be hard, full of unforeseen obstacles and darkness. Sometimes, it even feels as though God is not there. Thankfully, faith in God is not about a feeling. We often live out our faith as we walk together—stumbling, encouraging, and following the path to the Light.

Jesus, you are my light. Remind me of your presence in times of sunny goodness and in times of fear-filled darkness.

Lacking Wisdom

by Eva Burkholder

If you need wisdom, ask our generous God, and he will give it to you. He will not rebuke you for asking.

JAMES 1:5 (NLT)

"HOW DO YOU know how to be a good father?" my first-born son asked from the back seat of the car. "I don't think I'll be able to do a good job."

Taking advantage of this teachable moment with a captive audience, I replied, "When I brought you home from the hospital, my mother—your grandma—came to assist me. She had the rare opportunity to hold a newborn grandchild because she was home from the mission field at that time. One day, she found me weeping as I held you in my arms.

"In concern, she asked me what was wrong. Through my tears, I told her that I didn't know anything about raising a child. I wanted her to tell me what to do.

"She graciously put her arms around me and quoted a familiar verse: 'If you need wisdom, ask our generous God, and he will give it to you' (James 1:5 NLT). She then told me that in every step of raising the children God gave me, when I didn't know what to do, I could ask him for wisdom, and he would give it to me.

"I have followed her advice many times in attempting to instruct you and your brother. When the time comes, I'm confident God will help you be a good father if you ask him for wisdom."

"Our grandma really is a wise woman," my son added when I finished telling the story.

My mother's wisdom came from God. My prayer is that I picked up some of her wisdom and passed it on to my sons.

My friends, what are you facing today? Ask God for wisdom, and he will generously give it to you. And then you, too, can be wise.

Lord Jesus, I am so grateful that you are a God who invites my requests rather than rebuking me for them. Today, I lack wisdom, so I ask for it, trusting that you will give generously to me.

Loving Power

by Eva Burkholder

———●◉●———

*May you experience the love of Christ, though it is too great
to understand fully. . . . Now all glory to God, who is able,
through his mighty power at work within us, to accomplish
infinitely more than we might ask or think.*

EPHESIANS 3:19–20 (NLT)

I LIKE TO WATCH *Star Trek*. Yes, I admit it, but I can hardly
help it with a house full of men. In an early episode of *The
Next Generation* TV series, Commander Riker receives supernat-
ural powers. He wants to prove that he can use those powers for
good by giving his friends their greatest wishes. As he starts to make
Wesley—a teenager—into an adult, give Geordi—a blind man—
his sight, and supply Data—an android—with human emotions,
they beg him to stop. They do not want his "gifts" because in the
long run, his power doesn't actually improve their lives.

Riker's power made me consider God's omnipotence. While
God has the power to do anything, he often doesn't exercise that
power in a way that seems logical to me. If he is truly all-powerful,
then how do I explain why loved ones die of cancer or why people hate and kill others? How do I answer my children's questions
when they see disasters on the evening news?

If I concentrate only on God's power to do things—especially
things that benefit me—I am left with a God who *could* act on my

behalf, but *doesn't*, so he looks capricious or mean. However, if I look at his power in conjunction with his goodness, mercy, wisdom, love, and holiness, I see that he will do what is best for me and what fits into his sovereign plan.

God is good. He loves me so much, and he will always act for my good. I can ask him to protect me, and he does. It might not happen as I imagine, but he will always use his power to act in my best interest.

I need this reminder today as I call on God's power—the same power that raised Jesus from the grave—to change lives, to change myself. But when God doesn't seem to act as powerfully as I beg him to, I find that *how* he acts turns out to be the best thing in the end.

Do you tend to focus more on God's omnipotence or his love?

Father God, teach me how to balance your omnipotence and your love. Help me to accept the mystery of your complexity. Thank you that you are all-powerful but that your power is always tempered and framed in your magnificent love for me.

Thermal Strength

by Becki James

⸺●◉●⸺

But those who trust in the LORD will find new strength.
They will soar high on wings like eagles. They will run
and not grow weary. They will walk and not faint.

ISAIAH 40:31 (NLT)

I PANTED, PACING STRIDES as sweat streaked my cheek. Yanking off my cap, I flapped wildly. Another gnat drew blood. *It's not much farther—just through the canopy of tall pines.* Booting some briars, I trampled the undergrowth to cross into the woods. At least it was cooler. Within a few steps, the gnats settled, and the sun haloed the treetops, casting channels onto the forest floor. Silence reverberated in a mesmerizing sound, feathering through the highest branches as the breeze elongated alto tones on every swoop.

Ahead, I recognized the moss-covered boulders. I scaled the spongy shroud with care to avoid slipping. Last leg heaved, I perched on top. The view was worthwhile. On the edge of the tree line, hanging over the precipice, stood an age-old pine called the *super canopy*. Nestled in its fork was one of the largest nests in the world—an *aerie*—fortress of the mighty eagle. Spanning six-feet wide by ten-feet deep, it was a formidable shelter.

I sat, transfixed by the nest's enormity and then by the

enormity of God. When torrents raged in my life, he sheltered me under his wings.

I raised my binoculars to witness this glorious eagle, adjusting the wheel until I spotted her wide-plank wings rising on thermals. She soared effortlessly, using wind to her advantage, like a secret flight elevator. Although her wingspan neared eight feet, she never dipped, just mounted higher and higher. But soon, the work would begin and she'd dive up to seventy-five miles per hour to snatch prey far below. I lowered my field glasses. *Hmm—she's resting.*

I turned toward the nest. It provides shelter but cannot sustain life. Eventually, the eagle must leave to hunt. From two miles up, she can spot prey, but it is still far away. If she maintains rhythmic flapping, she'll weary. And, if she hits her target, home is still aloft. The task is laborious. But God provides thermals for flight and a nest for sanctuary.

I pondered my own strength. How often have I wearied myself by overlooking God's presence? How many times have I taken flight, overextending myself, only to drop under the load? At times, I have fainted in fear, afraid to fully trust God. He provides strength for the eagle, gifting her the warm embrace of the wind. He also promises to provide new strength to me when I trust him. In the nest or mid-flight, he supplies the shelter and thermals I need. When I trust him, I will walk, I will run, and I will soar.

Father, I'm weary. I'm struggling. I need new strength. I trust myself to the warmth of your wind as you guide the details of my life. Thank you for the shelter of your presence.

Give Me Your Hand

by Darla S. Grieco

---

*"Truly, I say to you, unless you turn and
become like children, you will never
enter the kingdom of heaven."*

MATTHEW 18:3 (ESV)

A S I CRESTED the hill to the elementary school parking
lot, rays of sunshine bled through the trees, flooding my
field of vision. Knowing the lot would be filled with parents and
small children, I slammed on my brakes. I carefully maneuvered
into the first spot I could find.

I wasn't the only one having trouble seeing that morning.
While I unloaded my son from the back seat, I heard a little voice
wail, "Mommy, I can't see anything!"

I turned to see a young boy about the age of six or seven
standing in the middle of traffic, shielding his eyes with his arms.

Thankfully, cars had stopped in both directions.

His mother's calm voice came out of nowhere, reassuring
him. "Give me your hand. I'll lead you."

Without any doubt or hesitation, the little guy reached out
and grabbed hold of his mother's outstretched hand, trusting that
she would lead him to safety.

I hate to admit it, but sometimes I'm less like this little boy than I would like to be. When I'm blinded by the world's circumstances and challenges, I tend to think I can manage the situation on my own. I hesitate to trust God with something I think I could probably get through just fine. Meanwhile, right in front of me, his hand is outstretched, waiting for me to receive his offer of help. "Give me your hand. I'll lead you."

Trust can be hard when we've grown up and seen so much heartache in life. But we must remember that God has our best interests at heart. He never leaves or forsakes us and would never lead us into dangerous circumstances.

I can see why Jesus said his kingdom belongs to the little children. They display innocence and a trust that is pure and unwavering. Never questioning. Never hesitating.

May I always remember that I can extend my hand and trust God to safely lead me.

Lord, restore my heart to that of a little child.
May I have unwavering trust in you with every
step I take today and forevermore.

Perspective

by Mindy Cantrell

———◦◉◦———

For I am about to do something new. See, I have already begun! Do you not see it? I will make a pathway through the wilderness. I will create rivers in the dry wasteland.

ISAIAH 43:19 (NLT)

*G*AZED OUT MY window with my county's stay-at-home order in place. Enjoying a few moments of reflection, my winter-weary soul drank in the new, green, budding life. Everywhere my eyes touched, I viewed a promise of beautiful life yet to come.

Tears built in my eyes as I thought of COVID-19 rampaging around the world, stealing precious life. I thought of our economy, the individuals and businesses struggling to survive in the midst of the lockdown. Sadness enveloped me. Fear grew in the hollow of my stomach.

The window beckoned me again. The beautiful, bright green buds bursting forth broke through my heartache and tears. The sun's soft rays warmed me as they shone through the window. I heard a whisper through my soul, and thankfulness bloomed in my heart for this promise—*this virus will not last forever. Life will bud and bloom again.*

As I took in the spring-awakened landscape across the front yard, my eyes fell on an imp sitting on the tree outside my window. His dark eyes stared directly at me. I jolted as *"Eek!"* escaped my lips.

Once my fright subsided, I laughed out loud. This little squirrel picked the teeniest branch from which to hang—the only one on the whole lower tree trunk. As he sat there, balancing just a few feet away from me, he seemed relaxed and without fear while he took it all in.

What perspective this little imp brought. It was as if he imparted this insight:

"Take time to appreciate the beauty around you, being thankful for what you have. Acknowledge those who need your prayers, and be diligent to pray for them. Do what you can to help them and to make a difference in the lives around you.

"But don't let the sorrows of the world bring you down into discouragement. Know that there is hope. New life will spring forth, even in the midst of a dark season."

Just as this cute little squirrel found the one tiny branch to hold him, you can find a tiny branch of hope to hold you.

Seek it. Find it. Step out onto it. Hold on to the hope it gives. And once you get your balance, share that hope with those around you. Take time to laugh out loud—it is such good medicine for your soul!

Dear heavenly Father, please open my eyes to see
the beauty and new life you create in and around me.
Give me courage to step out onto your branch of hope
as I learn to let go and trust you more.

The Measure of a Performance

by Lori Lipsky

*Therefore encourage one another and
build one another up.*

1 Thessalonians 5:11 (esv)

HOW INSPIRING TO see the courage that emerges from a few reassuring words. It's often evident during recital season. Twice a year at the music school where I teach, my piano students participate in a weekend recital. Because of the size of the school, we host nine recitals throughout a weekend to accommodate all who want to participate.

It takes courage for students to play piano in a large room before an audience. For some students, it's more of a challenge than others. I used to struggle with fear prior to my performances, even in college. I remember what a difference a kind comment can make.

During their lessons after the recital, I ask students how they think their performances went. They usually focus on the negative. I hear comments such as these:

"I made two mistakes on the first page and one on the second."

"I missed a couple of rests, especially that important one near the end. I was so embarrassed."

"I started too fast. I should have started slower."

Sometimes I share the story of a figure skating competition I watched on television years ago. One of the top-ranked men tried several difficult jumps. He fell twice during his routine. At the end of the performance, the panel of judges didn't disqualify him. Instead, they congratulated him on his overall performance and its level of difficulty by awarding him a high score. He fell down on the ice twice, but he won the competition.

Life is like a recital solo or a skating performance. We hit a wrong note. We fall on the ice. But the Judge of the universe encourages us, often through the words of others.

On life's journey, we make plenty of mistakes. Sometimes our mistakes are just blunders. Sometimes they're because of sin. We sin. Those around us sin. But once we confess and ask for forgiveness, it's good to move forward, rather than dwell on past mistakes or the mistakes of others.

Perhaps you have an encourager in your life who uses words to build you up. I hope you do. What might we say to encourage someone today? How can we use our words to build another up?

Lord, please nudge me when people in my life would benefit from a positive comment. Give me the words to say. Equip me to be an encourager.

Stand Still and Be Sad

by Eva Burkholder

And he said to them, "What is this conversation
that you are holding with each other as you
walk?" And they stood still, looking sad.

LUKE 24:17 (ESV)

I FEEL SAD. SAD that so many are dying from viruses and cancer. I grieve. My life has been so upended. I mourn over the strife between families and neighbors and cry for those who experience injustice.

Two of Jesus's disciples experienced this same sense of sadness. After their rabbi's tragic death on a cross and all hopes of a new earthly kingdom dashed, they took a walk together on the Emmaus road. I imagine their conversation was much like mine these days—full of grief, anxiety, confusion, and all they missed.

Jesus then joined their discussion. The verse records a simple phrase packed with meaning, "They stood still, looking sad." These guys got it!

Sometimes, I just have to stand still and be sad. I won't stay here forever. But I need to remain here for a while because it is both okay and necessary to be sad in order to grieve well. Therapists tell me that I need comfort during times of grief. Jesus comforted the two men by simply being there with understanding and love. He did not attempt to fix or change the situation. Not saying a word, he comforted with his presence. In other words, comfort says, "That's horrible. I'm so sorry. I feel sad with you. That sounds really hard. It's okay to cry."

Even if no one else offers me comfort, Jesus himself stands with me in my sadness. He knows my sorrow and comforts me with his presence as he did for the men on the road that day.

I know there are many things God is doing behind the scenes, and one day, I will look back and recount those. But for now—for today—I need to stand still and be sad.

What is making you sad today? How might God be comforting you?

Jesus, our Savior, I am sad. My world is sick and hurting. Your creation groans. Everyone around me has severe needs. Thank you for standing with me and giving me permission to be sad. Hear my cries and bring comfort with your presence.

Excellent Design

by Charlaine Martin

———●◆●———

For you formed my inward parts; you knitted me together in my
mother's womb. I praise you, for I am fearfully and wonderfully
made. Wonderful are your works; my soul knows it very well.

PSALM 139:13–14 (ESV)

OH, NO! I thought, sorting through a new rack of colorful
shirts. This shirt had a slash, as did the rest. Excited about
new clothing that came into our store, I rushed from my register
on lunch to find a couple of work outfits. These shirts caught my
eye because they were inexpensive and came in several colors, but
they were ruined. How disappointing. I reported it to the depart-
ment manager, ate my lunch, and then dashed back to my register.

Greeting customers with a smile as I rang up their purchases,
a cloudy turmoil churned inside me. Somehow, I often felt like
those shirts—damaged goods no one would want. That notion was
far from the truth. My husband loved me. Our families loved me.
So, what was responsible for this dark cloud? As I thought back to
my childhood, the mixed messages about myself from domestic
violence flooded back. I would never amount to anything. I was
ugly. I could not do anything right. Worthless.

Years later in life, I discovered several valuable truths. I am
God's beautiful creation. He loves me and has given me unique

gifts, talents, and abilities. Three years of Christian counseling helped me replace my past pain with this truth. Many other women who grew up in domestic violence struggle with the same feelings. Harsh words can deeply wound young hearts, which causes them to question their worth.

In Psalm 139, King David considers his value as God's creation. God intentionally designed David for a unique purpose in his kingdom. God never makes mistakes in his creation. Each person is intentionally valuable. When we consider our Bible passage in light of Jesus's death and resurrection, we come to understand this: we are God's excellent design deeply loved by him. We can replace the lies we heard from others about our value with truth from God's Word.

When you consider yourself and your life, what have you heard about your value from others? Does it align with God's truth about you? If so, appreciate this truth. If not, when negative thoughts about yourself come to mind, try reading this passage. Consider also your precious God-given traits and thank him for his loving, purposeful creation in you. Walk confidently in this truth. See how this truth applies to you, as well as those around you.

Lord, the words I heard from others in my past resound in my heart. Much of it does not come from you. I want to believe you about your love for me and the value you have given me. Show me your truth to replace the lies in my heart and help me see others through this same truth.

Thinking Ahead to
Serve Others

by Lori Lipsky

*And let us consider how to stir up one
another to love and good works.*

HEBREWS 10:24 (ESV)

PEOPLE PLAN FOR all sorts of things. We plan for vacations, weddings, and retirement. We set work goals, making lists of projects and tasks we need to tackle. People plan home cleaning routines. We plan meals ahead to save on trips to the grocery store. We plan so we're ready and prepared to the best of our ability.

Hebrews 10:24 tells us we're to think about how to encourage people to love others and do good. According to *Merriam-Webster's Unabridged Dictionary*, the word *consider* means "to think about carefully; to reflect; to deliberate."

I use lists for planning. My friends know I enjoy reading lists and making them. They've gifted me with list-making journals and books containing interesting lists made by others.

I've created lists of my favorite books, authors, and movies. I've made lists of the states and countries I've visited. I've written a list of my favorite television theme songs and a list of my life goals.

Sometimes I make to-do lists for my day. But I've never created a list to plan how I might encourage others toward love and good works.

As we live our lives as Christians, we sometimes fall into opportunities to build up the body of Christ. But the Bible says that the Lord wants us to go further. He wants us to give careful thought and to plan how we might use our influence. He tells us to take conscious aim, focusing on specific ways we might prompt others to do good. We're to motivate those within our sphere of influence. We're to plan how we might stimulate them to be involved in acts of kindness. Hebrews 10:24 exhorts us to invest ourselves for the sake of others and the body of Christ as a whole. God's Word urges us to pursue love and help others do the same. We're to give careful thought to such things and make plans.

Lord, I have not been created simply for my own purposes.
Please guide and equip me as I consider how I might
encourage others to pursue love and good deeds.

Truth—No Claws Needed!

by Nancy Graves

<hr/>

Sanctify them [purify, consecrate, separate them for Yourself, make them holy] by the Truth; Your Word is Truth.

JOHN 17:17 (AMPC)

A FEW YEARS AGO, we moved to a new house, and that's where the challenge began. But before I could unload the storage container, I found myself at a standstill. Most of the rooms were covered in wallpaper. Highly in vogue in the 70s, these colors and prints *had* to go. I'd never removed wallpaper, so—a complete noob—off to the store I went.

I read the product labels carefully. Each praised their miracle solution, touting near magic results. From steamers to toxic solvents, I weighed my options. Finally, I chose a spray solution guaranteed to nearly melt the paper off. First, the wall had to be scored with a tiger-like claw to perforate the paper, which would allow the solution to seep in. Paying a considerable amount for one bottle of magic and a claw, I headed home.

With great anticipation, I followed the claw directions, then sprayed liberally. Nothing happened. I waited for the all-important seeping. Nothing. I sprayed more solution—vigorously. Still nothing. Hoping to help the process along, I wedged my scraper between two seams and tried to lift the paper. Then I realized nothing was *ever* going to happen.

My visions of a proud DIY moment evaporated. The advertised miracle was nothing more than a deceptive marketing strategy. I'd been sold a bill of goods!

Finally, I gave up on my attempt and hired a professional. The man was a genius. He listened to my frustration and tried to assuage my guilty budgetary conscience by using the store product. But, he quickly made a wise executive decision. We would use what he knew worked best, a bucket of warm water and a sponge.

I was skeptical. How could mere water penetrate the non-porous membrane? How could plain H_2O soften the hardened glue that had held fast for decades?

Armed with spray bottles, sponges, and scrapers, we began dousing the walls. We tore a little here, a little there, scraped, then repeated the process.

Guess what happened? Magic! Huge sheets peeled off at a time. No claw marks, no furry surfaces, just clean drywall needing my perfect color selection. Again—genius—this man should write a book.

In reflection, I realized I'd sought truth in all the wrong places. I didn't know what I didn't know—and they knew that. Seeking wisdom from those who make a profit from my ignorance was foolish. I needed an expert.

Life is a lot like stripping wallpaper. What I need is *the* Expert, God. I need his book, the Bible. And I need a regular dousing of truth—the pure water of the Word of God. It strips away the sin and hardness of heart that has clung to me—sometimes for decades. And, take it from me, the more water, the better!

Dear Lord, please douse me in the truth of your Word.

The Kiss

by Sandy Lipsky

---

*If you really fulfill the royal law according
to the Scripture, "You shall love your
neighbor as yourself," you do well.*

JAMES 2:8 (NKJV)

*T*HE KISS I witnessed shocked me. I would never do that.

Old friends invited us to visit them in Texas. Their daughter attended a local university. They asked if our family would like to explore the campus. Seated in the back seat next to my daughter, I peered out the truck's side window. On the corner of the intersection where we had stopped for the traffic light, a group of college-aged young women waited to cross the street. Dressed up—perhaps for a girls' night out. The walk light flashed, and the gaggle began to cross. One lagged behind the others and caught my attention.

As her friends rushed to the other corner, I watched the blonde-headed co-ed bend at the waist to speak to a disheveled, wrinkled-faced person seated in a wheelchair. Man or woman, I couldn't tell. After the conversation, the lass stood and unzipped her wallet. She bent again to place something in the crippled hand. Her next action stunned me. The college student kissed the dirty, sunken cheek. Patting the skin where she had just placed her lips, she stood and smiled at the fragile soul. With a look and a wave, her attention turned back to her friends.

Settled back in my seat, I contemplated what I'd observed. This brief exchange was special. It was as if God lifted a veil, allowing me to witness a holy transaction. *That is what Jesus would have done*, I reflected. The beauty of this simple act of kindness etched itself forever in my mind.

In God's Word, we read that he doesn't look at a person's outward appearance but at the heart. This sacred moment allowed me to witness a heavenly example of how someone should treat a neighbor. No matter how a person appears on the outside, each is created in the image of God. Each is precious to him. As his child, I want to reflect my Father's love.

Father, I want to see people as you do. Allow me to be your hands and feet. Help me to love those you put in my path.

Shame Vests

by Sandy Lipsky

—————————————●◉●—————————————

*All of us, like sheep, have strayed away. We have
left God's paths to follow our own. Yet the LORD
laid on him the sins of us all.*

ISAIAH 53:6 (NLT)

WHAT IF YOU were made to wear a vest with your
personal sins written on it? Mine would read *idolater,
liar, disobedient, gluttonous,* to name a few.

My family and I were driving on curvy roads through the
mountains in a southern state when around a bend, I saw something that made my jaw drop. Several men stood on the side of
the highway, picking up trash. Each soul wore a neon orange vest
with the following message emblazoned across his back: "I AM
A DRUNK DRIVER." In bold letters, the sin each committed
shouted at all who drove by. As I read the offense of each man, I
began to weep. Sin is ugly. It is not private.

What if I had to wear my sin on a vest? I would feel shame.
Overwhelming shame! Hopeless and worthless, like human trash.

In the Bible, God's requirement for sin is death. Because he
loves us so much, God sent his only Son to pay what we owed.
Seeing each prisoner branded with his sin made me thankful for
forgiveness. Jesus bore the sins of the world, which includes those

men wearing their shame vests. Elvina Hall penned these words, "Jesus paid it all, all to him I owe. Sin has left a crimson stain. He washed it white as snow."

We all wear shame vests, don't we? Invisible, but they are there. For everyone who accepts Jesus Christ as Lord and Savior, he lifts off the vest of shame and places it on himself. I'm so glad I came to faith in him many years ago. In exchange, he covers us with a new, pure vest of righteousness. Hallelujah!

Thank you, Father, for sending your Son to die on the cross for my sins. He took on my shame vest so I could be pure. Praise you for the forgiveness and new life you give me through Jesus Christ, your beloved Son. I rejoice that he conquered sin and death and now sits at your right hand.

Unfinished Tasks

by Eva Burkholder

———— ◦●◦ ————

All these people died still believing what God had promised
them. They did not receive what was promised, but they
saw it all from a distance and welcomed it.

HEBREWS 11:13 (NLT)

I LOVE CROSSING THINGS off my to-do lists—unwanted
tasks as well as life-giving ones written on notepads and sticky
notes. Done. Finished. Wrapped up. Nice and neat. List tossed in
the trash. While some of my friends enjoy the work process, I find
more delight in the completion. Only then can I rest.

However, this creates a problem for me because rarely do I
ever get to the end of the list. On most days, a few items even get
carried over to a new list when the note has no more blank space.
Because so much remains incomplete, I live in limbo. I wait for
the email to arrive, the conference to be over, the casserole to bake,
the check-out line to dwindle, for . . . for . . . And so, I don't rest.

A plaque on my shelf by Fanny Crosby reminds me of my
goal, "Live in the moment and make it so beautiful that it will
be worth remembering." I realize I believe the myth that I cannot
experience contentment while I juggle so many balls or wait to
finish a task.

In search of an answer to the unrest in my soul today, I turn to the example of Abraham and Sarah. They died without receiving all the things God promised. Talk about an unfinished task that never got crossed of their list! So how do I reframe this unsettledness? I keep reading in Hebrews:

> And let us run with endurance the race God has set before us. We do this by keeping our eyes on Jesus, the champion who initiates and perfects our faith. Because of the joy awaiting him, he endured the cross, disregarding its shame. . . . Think of all the hostility he endured from sinful people; then you won't become weary and give up. (Hebrews 12:1–3 NLT)

I choose to focus on Jesus, not the lists. To consider his sacrifice and endurance to help me not grow weary and give up. To remember that true rest is found in Jesus and not my crumpled note in the trash.

What unfinished task remains on your list? How does Jesus's example of endurance encourage you while you wait?

Jesus my Savior, thank you for enduring with joy so that I can know true rest in you. I don't need to strive to accomplish my tasks to gain approval from you or contentment for my soul. You have already given me that. Teach me to persevere in the mundane, but also to look toward you with faith.

Women's Issues

Reward Wife

by Sandy Lipsky

*Live happily with the woman you love through all the
meaningless days of life that God has given you under the sun.
The wife God gives you is your reward for all your earthly toil.*

ECCLESIASTES 9:9 (NLT)

*H*OW DO YOU feel about surprises? I love good ones! My
husband gave me a new and bigger diamond ring for our
anniversary. It was one of the best surprises of my life. A recent
phone call I received from a high-school friend I hadn't seen in
many years was another.

I delight in surprises from God's Word, too. One day, a
Scripture passage I'd read multiple times in the past burst forth
from the page like a jack-in-the-box. This verse grabbed my
attention during a time of sorrow in our family. My husband
and I had each lost a parent within a few months of one another.
We stumbled through many months tired, sad, and burned out.
Wondering on this morning if I would ever experience happiness
again, I flipped to the book of Ecclesiastes. I stopped reading when
I came to Ecclesiastes 9:9.

Me? A reward?

My inner voice over the years shouted "loser" with regularity.

The affirmation *reward* awakened a sleeping hope and stirred a dormant joy in my spirit.

Looking up definitions, even of familiar words, helps illuminate Scripture passages for me. Pulling out my old high school dictionary, I read the following: a reward is "something given or received in recompense for worthy behavior" (*The American Heritage Dictionary*).

For my husband's hard toil and work, this Scripture said he was gifted with a wife.

God, through his Word, showed me the truth. My self-talk was wrong and needed an adjustment. I am not a loser. I am a reward. God is clear. We wives are a prize!

Show me, Father, what it looks like to be a reward.
Help this truth to transform the way I look at myself
and act toward my husband. Open my eyes and ears
to his needs. Equip me to be his reward wife.

One Harvest at a Time

by Darla S. Grieco

———◦●◦———

And let us not grow weary of doing good, for in
due season we will reap, if we do not give up.

GALATIANS 6:9 (ESV)

ECOMING A STAY-AT-HOME mom had never been a
goal of mine, but somehow, that is exactly where I found
myself. Though I had earned two degrees and held a successful
job during my early twenties, my lot now included mounds of
laundry, dirty dishes, and screaming children—four of them, to be
exact. When possible, I tried to participate outside of my home,
either at church or in the children's schools, but as demands with
the kids increased, all other activities faded away. Gradually, I lost
sight of who I was. I often wondered if I even mattered outside of
my roles at home. Did I make a difference in this world?

Then, one day, I chaperoned a fifth-grade field trip with my
daughter. One of the other mothers approached me, eyeing me
closely. "I know you," she said.

She looked familiar, but I couldn't recall where I'd seen her
before. We went over our litany of frequented places—the bank,
places of employment, church. Nothing.

The day drifted on, but we could not figure out how or where we'd crossed paths. I often caught her staring, a perplexed look on her face. But then, she'd shake her head and look away puzzled.

That was, until we stood by a trickling stream, watching the children search for salamanders. Suddenly, Beth turned and pointed a finger in my direction. "Isaiah 54:5!" she shouted.

"Excuse me?" I said.

"You gave me that Scripture. You know, the one about 'Your Maker is your husband —the Lord of hosts is his name—and the Holy One of Israel is your Redeemer; the God of the whole earth he is called.'" (Isaiah 54:5 esv)

I stood there, blinking at her. Waiting.

"I came to your house for Bible studies," she motioned toward our daughters, now fifth graders, "when these two were babies."

Fighting tears, I listened as Beth continued to tell me how that Scripture I shared with her so many years ago carried her through a difficult season in her life.

"I treasure it to this day," she said.

It occurred to me that almost a decade had passed, but something I said touched her life. She appreciated it. She appreciated me, confirming that I did have a purpose.

Throughout my life, I've planted many seeds. This time, God gave me a glimpse of how one seed had grown.

While we cannot always see the fruit of our labor, God can and will bless our efforts. I didn't need a corporate job or to speak before masses of people to affect someone. I could be of service right where I was, one person at a time.

Lord, thank you for using my efforts for your glory, whether I see the outcome or not. Please continue to use me right where I am.

Too Much from the Wrong Man

by Darla S. Grieco

For am I now seeking the approval of man, or of God?
Or am I trying to please man? If I were still trying to
please man, I would not be a servant of Christ.

Galatians 1:10 (esv)

"*Y*OU'RE TOO MUCH!" the man I loved said. Then he shook his head in annoyance and stormed off.

When our relationship started, I thought he loved me. It didn't take long for me to notice each time he used that phrase, the word *much* referred to an endless list of ways I fell short of his expectations. What he really meant was, "You're too weak. You're unaccomplished. You're messy. You're irritating." These were all words spewed at me from an unloving place.

Unfortunately, though, I allowed his words to take up residency in my heart. I developed a fresh script—a way of speaking to myself—that included his negative messages about me. In my heart, I came to believe they were all true, and I scrambled endlessly, attempting to please him.

Then, one day at my lowest point, I flipped open my Bible. There before me, I saw God's words. His script throughout various passages of the Bible told me: *You are fearfully and wonderfully made. . . . The apple of my eye. . . . I love you so much that I sent my Son to die for you despite your flaws.*

I had known those concepts appeared in the Bible, but finally, that day, God's words stole my heart. I realized it was time to replace the script I'd learned from an earthly man with God's beautiful truths about me.

Yes, I may be disorganized at times and allow the floors to stay dirty for a few days too long. Occasionally, I forget to send off paperwork I'm supposed to, or I may laugh a little too loud in public. I might leave my shoes and work bag by the door where they don't belong or serve Cheerios for dinner.

But none of these faults define me, and none can replace or rewrite the truth that exists about who I am in Christ.

Even in our moments when we are "too much" for someone's earthly standards, God sees those as temporary flaws, human moments of weakness. If anything, he comes alongside us in those situations, picks us up, and resurrects our spirits, for he loves us with an undeniable, unshakeable love.

So much so that he sent his Son to die for you and me.

Lord, remind me to take the feedback I get from this world to you. May you help me see what is true and what is not. May I value your opinion above all else.

Unfulfilled Dreams

by Diana Leagh Matthews

———◉◉◉———

*"Sing, O barren one, who did not bear; break forth into
singing and cry aloud, you who have not been in labor!
For the children of the desolate one will be more than the
children of her who is married," says the LORD."*

ISAIAH 54:1 (ESV)

*H*AVE YOU EVER wanted something so badly you could
taste it? And then it never happened?

Growing up, I had the same dream as most little girls to
become a wife and mother one day. This was my greatest hope and
desire.

Fast forward more than three decades, and it remains an un-
answered prayer and desire. After two ill-chosen and abusive hus-
bands, I'm still single and childless. There are times when my heart
breaks over the loss of this unfulfilled dream and the loneliness
that emanates.

On more than one occasion, I have pushed back the tears as
I hold a newborn baby or sat through a Mother's Day service at
church. I've found it easy to cry out to God. *Why not me? What did
I do wrong? Please help me!*

Time and again, the Lord leads me to the verse about a barren
woman having more children than a mother with children. This

metaphor for Jerusalem and the Jews inspires me even though it's not about a woman, but a nation.

The Lord revealed to me that while I may not have children of my own, he's placed me in that role throughout my life. In college, I was the mother figure to our group of friends. As a young adult, I worked with youth in the church and taught music. Today, I work with youth volunteers, senior adults, and those with disabilities in a nursing home setting.

While I have no children of my own, I've had many children to influence—of all different ages and creeds.

Even when we don't understand or even like the Lord's answer, he is faithful and will provide. Is there an area of your life that God didn't answer the way you envisioned?

Heavenly Father, thank you for the opportunity to minister to others in a variety of capacities and ways. Even when I don't understand or like the answer, you are always faithful. Help me keep my eyes and heart on you. Soothe this burning desire within my soul. You are the Alpha and Omega and the lover of my soul. Thank you for loving me. Use me for your honor and glory.

Repositioning the Flock

by Edna Earney

———•◦◗◦•———

Shepherd the flock of God that is among you, exercising oversight, not under compulsion, but willingly, as God would have you; not for shameful gain, but eagerly; not domineering over those in your charge, but being examples to the flock.

1 PETER 5:2–3 (ESV)

M Y ARMS PRICKLED with goosebumps, my spine tingled—all those signs of *Aha! Yes!* This response happened when my friend Kelly said, "If you ever teach a literature class to adults, I want in." I felt God pitching a literary book club to me, and my body alerted my excitement.

A month later, surrounded by friends and former students, Good Books, Better Friends was born. We sat at a large table in a local coffee shop to discuss our first book choice, *Wuthering Heights* by Emily Bronte. Kelly had a puzzled look when I used the term *character foils*. Her puzzlement turned to a satisfied smile when she heard me explain foils as characters with opposite personalities or values. She offered the example of Saul and David in their pursuit of God. I smiled and nodded. She relaxed her shoulders, sat back, and grinned, "Yes. Got it." This was exactly what Kelly wanted—to learn to read deeper literature as an adult learner. And I still get to enjoy teaching!

We laughed as some members talked about how much they disliked the book and others relished it. We compared the conflicts of mother Catherine and her daughter Cathy, swooned with Cathy and Heathcliff's star-crossed love, and pitied poor, neglected Hareton. Kelly, and others, let me know when hearing a literary device for the first time. Their pleasure in learning was obvious. We soaked in the friendships created between former students and my older lady friends and enjoyed immersing ourselves in the discussion. I confess I had a couple of teary moments. *These former students want to sit with their old, retired English teacher and discuss old books. Wow.*

The next day Kelly said, "God has called you to continue your gift to a broader audience including the young and the old, the saved and the unsaved, spanning the past, present, and future. You are not in retirement. You are repositioned to continue his work." *Goosebumps, again.*

May we all be like Kelly, encouraging an old friend in a new stage of life. Or like those former students who still want the enrichment of reading to stir their imaginations. Or maybe the surprised teacher, warmed in her elder years by the love of relationship and humbled to have "her flock" repositioned.

Our most excellent Teacher, help me as the years turn to know that you will bring new pursuits and teach me new ways to use my talents. Thank you for moments that enrich me, fulfill me, and give me the courage to continue in your work.

Why Do I Talk Too Much?

by Mary E. Curcio

He will rejoice over you with gladness, He will quiet you with his love.

Zephaniah 3:17 (nkjv)

WHY AM I such a talker? My mom says I was born talking. Why couldn't I stop talking? I often asked the Lord why but never seemed to get an answer.

Guilt plagued me for years. I often felt uncomfortable when I couldn't stop talking. As a teacher, it's my job. Can you imagine a teacher who doesn't speak? Still, I wondered why I talked too much.

I never took my "talking problem" seriously until one day, I overheard someone discussing me. They complained that I was annoying and talked too much. I grieved over those words, but it prompted me to get serious about "being a talker."

Life growing up was difficult. Living in the suburbs of Boston, we were very poor. When I was a young child, my dad was murdered. This was a stigma for a child in the fifties. To this day, I still feel the pain of being on the playground and children making fun of me. On top of that, I was obese. I lacked confidence and self-esteem.

As I reflected on my past, I began talking to the Lord about my talking. The Holy Spirit revealed my insecurities. I never felt safe. Even though I had a loving family and husband, I didn't feel loved. I always had to please everyone. I worried about how others felt about me. I never dealt with my emotional wounds, nor did I want to. I decided I was not going to let those wounds haunt me anymore.

I loved God's Word and knew if I was going to use my words less, I would have to depend on his words more. Daily, I studied the scriptures but didn't find an answer until I stumbled upon that one verse. A verse that broke my heart when I realized I didn't know God's love, nor did I know how to love. This was the root of my emotional wounds.

Like a skilled surgeon, the Lord peeled back layers of emotional issues. As God's Word spoke to my spirit, I talked less. New revelations of God's love gradually replaced each emotional wound. Healing from God was slow and steady.

When you need healing, seek the Word. At times I still struggle with talking too much, but I am confident he continues to rejoice over me. There is no need to feel guilty about any emotional wounds you have. He will quiet you with his love.

Lord, I pray that you will forgive me when I talk too much. I pray that your words will be my words. I thank you for the assurance that you always love me, no matter what I am dealing with.

Losing Time

by Stephenie Hovland

*So teach us to number our days that we
may get a heart of wisdom.*

Psalm 90:12 (esv)

EVERY DAY I seemed to lose a few minutes. I kept checking my watch, but I still ended up being late to events (and I'm rarely late). The hands on my watch were slowing down, and I didn't realize it. I reset my watch, but the time was slow again and again—until I got a new watch.

Some days when I plan to read my Bible or go for a walk, I get to the end of the day and find that time is up. I didn't take time to study God's Word or get fresh air—again. The excuses are endless. I'll get to it after I fold laundry, after I check Facebook, after lunch . . . Finally, I'm too tired, so I go to bed. I pull up the covers and realize I'm disappointed because I let everything else in my day take a bigger chunk of my time and energy than what I consider to be high priorities—my spiritual and physical health. How high of a priority can something be if I never make time to do it?

What choices in your life do you say are important but continue to ignore? Your health? Saving money? Reading your Bible? Think about what might help you put that priority at a higher level. Would it help to pray to God and tell a friend? Sometimes if you just ask yourself, "Why is this important?" and "Why do I keep skipping it?" you'll find some valuable answers. Often we need reminders because we focus on meeting others' needs and don't prioritize our own. Maybe you need more support, like a walking buddy or a Bible study partner. Ask God to help you put your priorities in order and give you some solid solutions. Then, do it! You won't regret the extra effort of putting your time and energy into what is important.

Dear heavenly Father, I know you value order and command us not to put other things in our lives ahead of you. Please forgive me when I let other things take priority over my responsibilities and my time with you.

Be the Friend

by Gina Stinson

*Therefore encourage one another and build one
another up, just as you are doing.*

1 Thessalonians 5:11 (esv)

THAT WOMAN YOU think has it all together? She doesn't. The one whose kids are dressed to the nines and never have a hair out of place—she's frazzled. The one with the humorous response or sarcastic remark—she's hurting. The lady who has a food-stained t-shirt and disheveled hair is barely hanging on. The wife who looks like she is perfectly perfect in every way—she's far from it. The one who has the office job that pays the big bucks—she lacks in other ways. The homeschooling mom—she's about ready to pull her hair out some days. Whatever your mental picture is of the woman who has it all together, forget about it. She doesn't exist.

Far too long, we've been intimidated by those whose lives look neat on the outside. Let's face this fact together—with pandemics, parenting, natural disasters, and whatever the rest of life is going to bring—nobody has it all together.

Most days, I tackle life with a messy bun and no makeup. I serve up more frozen pizza and burgers than I am comfortable admitting. The house is wrecked a couple of times a week, and I wonder if I am making a difference.

This is where most people live.

We live in the middle places. We wonder if we are good enough. We wish for friendship but doubt our worth. We question what God was thinking when he chose us to be a wife or mother. We know we need something but doubt we have the time for it. We dress up for work or church but deep down inside know it's all just a big farce. We contemplate our gifting and challenge our callings.

I don't know about you, but I need other strong women around me. Naomi had Ruth. Mary had Martha. Jesus's mother, Mary, had Elizabeth. Each relationship brought them closer to one other and to the Lord.

I need others to remind me of who I am. I need others to jerk me back to reality when I dive into disparities. I need others to encourage me, correct me, and laugh with me. I need others to listen, love me, and support me.

I need a lot.

But so do you. Let's be there for each other—to walk together. Let's give each other the benefit of the doubt. Let's love each other in the middle—the middle of snotty-nosed kids, pandemics, homeschooling, financial problems, child-raising, young-adult parenting. In the middle of questioning our faith, wondering about the future, worrying for our kids and for our nation. In the middle of hot flashes and mood swings and hysterectomies and cancer and death.

God gave us each other. Be there. Love each other.

That's what I need. I bet you do too.

Be the friend you wish you had.

Superheroes

by Joanie Shawhan

───────●◉●───────

*A capable, intelligent, and virtuous woman—who is he who
can find her? She is far more precious than jewels . . . She
opens her mouth in skillful and godly Wisdom, and on her
tongue is the law of kindness [giving counsel and instruction].*

PROVERBS 31:10, 26 (AMPC)

*T*HEME NIGHT AT my ovarian cancer camp featured
superheroes. Larger than life, the Incredible Hulk, Batman,
Spiderman, Superman, and Wonder Woman lined the dining
hall. We laughed and posed in our real and imagined superheroes
costumes against backdrops of the Hall of Justice, the Heroes
Lounge, the Enemy's Lair, and a telephone booth. Cloaked in
teal, we were transformed into caped crusaders focused on our
mission—to fight ovarian cancer.

I'm not sure I've ever outgrown my need for superheroes. At
various stages of my life, I've sought out those trailblazers whose
example encouraged me and offered me hope.

God provided a long list of superheroes in his Word—
heroes of the faith—women empowered by God to overcome
insurmountable obstacles. Esther risked her life to save her people.
Deborah, a judge of Israel, defeated enemy armies. Hannah poured
out her heart to God, and he answered her prayers with the birth
of Samuel. Mary said yes to the angel, for nothing is impossible

with God. Through their struggles and victories, the courage of these women stirs my faith.

God has not only given me biblical superheroes, but he also provided superhero women in my life. These women don't wear capes or leap off buildings. Nonetheless, they've directed me and even rescued me from potential harm with their godly wisdom and insight. They are ordinary women who have overcome adversity—women of faith who have walked alongside me, prayed for me, and shared their insights to mentor me in my weakness. They offer their strength, support, love, and encouragement, as well as a listening ear—one ear tuned in to me and the other ear tuned in to God.

Their example has enabled me to offer this support and encouragement to other women.

My heroes of faith appear in all shapes and sizes. They are everyday women who have faced challenges and overcome adversity, clothed with strength, dignity, and joy.

Lord, thank you for the women of faith you have placed in my life who encourage me, pray for me, and offer me hope during seasons of adversity. Help me, Lord, to provide this same support to other women.

Rest for a Weary Soul

by Charlaine Martin

And He said to them, "Come aside by yourselves to a deserted place and rest a while." For . . . they did not even have time to eat. So they departed to a deserted place in the boat by themselves.

Mark 6:31–32 (NKJV)

*M*Y PHONE BUZZED in my pocket. My elderly mom's voice wavered, "Char, can you pick me up from the hospital?" Why was she there? She fell again, for the second time in two weeks. *Sigh.* I had looked forward to flying our single-engine plane, taking in the stunning Great Lakes scenery from the sky. Mom needed me, yet I needed a getaway. I felt pulled in several directions. Instead, I gave that time and energy to take Mom home, settle her into her apartment, and figure out plan B. I was torn.

On the one hand, I resented any intrusion on time with my husband and enjoying God's splendid artwork. But on the other hand, I felt worried and guilty. Why did she fall again? What if she continues to fall? Why am I resentful? Since her needs took most of our day, we took a nature walk with the remaining daylight available instead of flying as we hoped. The glories of God shone in the brilliant reds, oranges, and yellows painted across the landscape. Fallen leaves rustled beneath our feet as we walked along the leaf-carpeted path, gently shaded by the tree canopy above. I desperately needed this rest.

Similarly, Jesus's disciples needed rest from their work. His disciples ministered non-stop and had not even eaten. When they came back from Jesus's assignment, they were exuberant about what God had done. Jesus recognized their exhaustion, so he told them, "Come aside by yourselves to a deserted place and rest a while" (Mark 6:31 NKJV). Even Jesus took rest breaks during his ministry by going to lonely places far from the crowds.

As a wife, mother, ministry leader, and personal trainer, I often tell God, "I am so exhausted." I tried burning the candle at both ends, often lighting a wick in the middle. God taught me that rest is essential to continue doing his work. Do you feel like this?

Burnout is imminent if we do not rest. Otherwise, we resent the very people God sends to us. Restoring your soul begins by spending time with Jesus. Sneak away for a moment of prayerful Bible reading. Go on a nature walk and take in God's glorious handiwork. Enjoy time with a relaxing hobby. Rest in the Lord to refresh your weary soul.

Thank you, Lord, for rest. I forget to take breaks when I help others. Please change my heart's attitude, so I don't resent the people you send to me. Restore my soul. Thank you for refreshing me to serve others well and glorify you.

Balancing My Busy

by Kristine Accola

The thief comes only in order to steal and kill and destroy. I came that they may have and enjoy life, and have it in abundance (to the full, till it overflows).

JOHN 10:10 (AMPC)

ARE YOU A multitasker? Multitasking sounds more efficient than just being busy. Being productive equals feeling accomplished. My daily performance often consists of juggling six balls in the air instead of three, dropping one, and having another hit me on the head as I bend down to retrieve it. So, is productivity and accomplishment really being achieved? Or is it an illusion because I'm busy?

We offer to help people. We volunteer for another project. We work a little overtime. None of these are bad things by themselves, but are we so busy doing good things that we neglect the best things? Like spending time with a friend, taking the kids ice skating, going to a spa, or taking a jog in the park for some self-care time. Most importantly, do we spend enough time with God?

When everything feels chaotic and out of sorts, it's because life's scales are out of calibration. One side of our scale is weighed down far too heavy, and the other side dangles. God gave us twenty-four hours in a day to handle the load of work, rest, and play. We get to choose how we divide those categories.

Sometimes being too busy leaves us *hanging* in the balance instead of *having* balance. It leaves us spinning out of control instead of being on an even keel. When we make God our top priority and we stop taking on more than 24/7 will allow, life feels calmer, and we feel more capable. We regain steadiness and are less flustered. We can better appreciate God's timing. We can do things we have to do without a bad attitude, and we can enjoy things we want to do without guilt.

Busyness is a thief. It steals time away from Jesus and others. It kills relationships and sours our goodwill toward men. It destroys our joy. God himself, the creator of the universe, took a day of rest, and he looked at all that he made and called it good. We are to trust God with our time and efforts, using both to glorify him. Occasionally, we need to just say no instead of, "Oooh, oooh, I will, pick me." Girl put that hand down!

Dear Jesus, help me to seek you first and to trust that everything will be accomplished at the right time. Help me make the most of each day and find a balance between the have-tos and the want-tos. Give me peace and clarity in all that I do, and let me do it all for you.

Retreat Doesn't Mean Defeat

by Kristine Accola

*Come to Me, all you who labor and are heavy-
laden and overburdened, and I will cause you to
rest. [I will ease and relieve and refresh your souls.]*

MATTHEW 11:28 (AMPC)

ARE YOU FEELING overwhelmed, worn out, a little out of
sorts with family or yourself? Are you being battered by
life's expectations? Do you poop out at parties? As I write this, I
realize this is me. I need to retreat. Again. It's an ongoing process.
Sometimes in the chaos and confusion of life and trying to do
everything myself, it gets to be too much. We were not created to
shoulder the burden of every little thing. God often reminds me
with a Bible verse, a TV program, or an inspirational song that I
need to let go—that he is the one in control.

Retreat means withdrawal, seclusion, refuge. It is a place
where you can regroup and reignite. God made a promise to hide
us, preserve us, and surround us with shouts of deliverance (Psalm
32:7).

When a soldier retreats, he isn't giving up, nor is he a coward.
He is securing a safe place where he can recharge and come up with
a different, better plan. We are soldiers in God's army. When we
retreat, it needs to be into his arms. We need to rest and recuperate

and seek his counsel. Offer prayers of gratitude instead of attitude. We are filled with complete peace when we rest in the Lord and surrender our battle to him. We obtain a fresh perspective and strength for each day. Leaning on Jesus leads to clarity, which then helps us make better decisions.

When storms rage and the power goes out, people scramble for flashlights or candles so they don't feel alone and out of control. Without God, we are alone and often out of control. We need to stay connected to God so that when the storms in our lives rage, we don't lose power and shut down. Ladies, let's react toward life with a grateful heart instead of a hateful heart. How do we stay connected with God? We simply spend more time with him by studying his Word or with worship and praise. Stay in touch with friends who lift you up and encourage you. Take some time just for yourself and count your blessings instead of your burdens.

Retreat is the opposite of defeat. It enables us to be victorious. It allows us to be refreshed, and it reignites the passion for our heavenly Father, our activities, and our relationships. Sign me up!

Lord, help me stay connected with you as I face life's challenges. Help me find a better balance in all the things that require my attention and rest in you when I feel overwhelmed. Reignite my spirit and let me be refreshed in you. I can't pour out if I don't fill up.

Finding Elusive Fruit

by Charlaine Martin

*But the fruit of the Spirit is love, joy, peace, longsuffering,
kindness, goodness, faithfulness, gentleness, self-control.
Against such things there is no law.*

GALATIANS 5:22–23 (NKJV)

M Y HUSBAND USED to hunt with his dad. He often
climbed a tree and shook down some fruit that many
people have never tasted—pawpaws. I was curious about this fruit,
so we searched for it on our nature walk this fall. Pawpaws, a del-
icate fruit that ripens in late autumn, does not ship well due to
easy bruising. It cannot be picked early to ship to stores, or it will
not ripen. Disappointed that we found none, we Googled them
to find the nearest place we could buy some—an hour-and-a-half
drive west.

One Saturday afternoon, we visited a large nursery that sells
pawpaw trees and the fruit. Excited, we chose a few ripe pieces and
paid the high price to try his special childhood treat. Their unique,
creamy texture and custardy mango-banana flavor delighted me.
Our grandson fell in love with them when he tasted one. Now I
want to grow our own.

Just as this fruit is little known, fragile, and ripens late in the
harvest season, so does the fruit of the Spirit. These nine character

traits of the Christian life are readily available to us as Christ-followers. Unfortunately, this fruit takes time to mature before we can share it with others. I struggle with the fruit of longsuffering, also known as patience. Much like the pawpaw, this fruit has taken a long time to grow, ripen, and be ready to share as a wife, mom, and grandma. I often pray for this difficult-to-obtain fruit to develop into maturity so that the people around me will benefit and, in turn, share with others.

You also have all nine of these Christian character traits available to you. Which one do you struggle to find or allow to mature in your own life, ready to share with others? Consider Christians you know who display this elusive fruit in their relationships. What are they doing differently in their faith walk that you can begin to emulate? Was it readily available for them, or did it take time to nurture and mature? Consider what you might need to let go of in your life to take hold of the spiritual fruit that seems out of reach. Prayerfully ask God to show you how you might experience the hard-to-find, attractive, yet fragile, spiritual fruit you seek. As it matures in your life, begin sharing it with the people around you.

Lord, thank you for making the fruit of the Spirit available to me. I struggle to see some of it in my attitudes and behaviors. Please, help me cultivate it to maturity and share it with others. May people see your character in my life.

Not Shaken

by Becki James

I have set the Lord always before me; because he is at my right hand, I shall not be shaken. Therefore my heart is glad, and my whole being rejoices; my flesh also dwells secure.

PSALM 16:8–9 (ESV)

MANY YEARS AGO, I lived through what I called my dark days. Although my love for the Lord flourished, circumstances beyond my control hovered like smoke over an inferno. Deep sadness set in as I watched pieces of my family collapse, shaken by the fires of chronic illness. I fought to restore joy, but the illness intensified at every turn, bringing clouds of discouragement. With no end in sight, uncertainty overshadowed our home. Years went by. Defeat lingered. My emotions wearied. Still, I loved the Lord and desperately wanted to serve him with gladness. At the same time, I questioned his purposes and struggled to hold on to hope.

The good news is hope cannot be consumed. It remains. But I had nothing left to offer anyone. My hope was scorched, then charred, and verged on disintegration.

Or was it?

Something happened. I heard God whispering—*My child, I am here*. Standing among the ashes, hope sprouted. I realized God's love for me was the foundation of my hope. He never failed me. He never left me. He was right beside me, but I was too focused on the fire to see him. I began tuning in to his presence, talking to him more throughout the day. I challenged myself to practice his presence, reminding myself that he was with me. That was the turning point. My perspective changed. I changed. Wildfires raged on but no longer consumed me. Contained within the perimeters of his purpose, their power over me diminished. My smile returned, and I felt a deeper confidence than ever before. The smoke eventually lifted, and I saw that he used those unwanted circumstances to refine my character and fan the flames of my faith.

The psalmist says he continually set the Lord in a position of importance, acknowledging his authority. Because of this, he was not shaken. God's love for me is why Jesus left his throne and endured the cross. That image steadied me. If he loved me that much, then I could not be shaken because I belonged to him. My dark days turned to ash, and I rejoiced in the light of my Savior.

Are fires shaking the foundations of your hope? Quench them with the security of God's presence. Give him room to rescue you by inviting him into every moment. Say with confidence, "The Lord is by my side and I will not be shaken."

Heavenly Father, I know that you are right beside me and that you love me. Help me focus on your love so that nothing has power to shake me. I trust your goodness. I rest in your love.

Sharing Life

by Lisa-Anne Wooldridge

———— •◉• ————

*We loved you so much that we shared
with you not only God's Good News but
our own lives, too.*

1 Thessalonians 2:8 (NLT)

$\mathcal{I}$ MOVED TO CALIFORNIA nearly a quarter of a century ago. I was a young newlywed with no friends in the area, excited to start a life with my husband in this faraway place where we both felt God wanted us to be.

I feared that we would be lonely or have trouble meeting people and making friends. I knew my husband would be very busy in his new job, so finding a community would fall on my shoulders. Thankfully, God already had a plan.

A kind group of church members—all of them about our parents' age—adopted us from the start. One couple came from South Africa, others were native Californians whose families had been there since the gold rush, and a few came for the Summer of Love in San Francisco but found Jesus and a new life. They were artists and woodworkers and entrepreneurs and financial planners and evangelists and IT workers, but they all had one thing in common: they felt it was important to share real life not just be "church friends."

They took us into their lives and homes for holidays and family dinners, and even on vacations. They queued up to be godparents to our children and looked after us during the most difficult time in our young lives when our son was born at only twenty-eight weeks. They helped us thrive in the storm, and when the storm lasted for years as our son struggled to survive and overcome, they stuck by us. And they let us do the same for them, whether it was house and child sitting, an early morning ride to the airport, or just being there with them as they lost family members to age or illness.

I grew up in the South, where we pride ourselves on hospitality, and we're good at it! Still, it can be hard to break into the tight-knit relationships built up over generations there. What I learned from my new West Coast family was another lesson in hospitality, one based on sharing life. An adopted family member shared a verse with me about how God sets the lonely into families on earth. I knew it was true. She told me that one day, in a different season of life, I would be the one noticing the lonely and adopting them the way she adopted me.

Twenty-five years later, I can say she was right. I'm still more likely to serve sweet tea than espresso, but now it's my turn to love people and include them in my family. In fact, it's one of my greatest joys.

Father, help me see the lonely and welcome them into my family. Help me love and include them the way you do.

Thank God for Chocolate Cake!

by Mindy Cantrell

But he answered, "It is written, "'Man shall
not live by bread alone, but by every word that
comes from the mouth of God.'"

Matthew 4:4 (esv)

*E*VER HAD ONE of those long days where no matter what you do, everything goes wrong? At the end of the day, if you're like me, you feel tired and discouraged. You just want your comfy pj's and dinner. But nothing sounds good—nothing that's good *for* you, anyway. Yes, you need a treat, something that will make you feel all better. Ah yes, comfort food.

You open the fridge and, *bam!* Right in front of your eyes is that dreamy chocolate cake left from last night's dinner. Mmm . . . rich, soothing, spirit-lifting, chocolate cake. Oh, thank God for chocolate cake!

But what do you do when there is no chocolate cake? How do you lift your spirits when your favorite comfort food is not available?

Having my daily quiet time provides the same comforting and satisfying feeling in my soul that chocolate cake gives after a bad day. It soothes my soul and all that ails it.

But, for me, just like that amazing chocolate cake, the right ingredients have to go into my quiet-time recipe. Without the main ingredient—rich, decadent chocolate—it just isn't chocolate cake, right?

In my quiet time, the main ingredient is God. Like chocolate, God's beautiful words of love and affirmation lift my spirits. They assure me that I am seen and heard—I am not alone. They tell me that, yes, I will have bad days along with the good. Because I was not made to be perfect, sometimes I will fail or do the wrong thing. But, because God is perfect, I can seek comfort in his presence as I learn from his Word how to do things better.

In Psalms, it says, "For you formed my inward parts; you knitted me together in my mother's womb. I praise you, for I am fearfully and wonderfully made. Wonderful are your works; my soul knows it very well" (Psalm 139:13–14 ESV). Here, we learn that God formed and made us from the very beginning and that all his works are wonderful. Wonderful! That means me. That means you. From the very beginning, we're all wonderful creations of God. And no amount of bad days or negative talk will ever take that truth away. We all have a wonderful foundation. We just have to reconnect with God to anchor ourselves to it again.

So, how about we go devour some rich, dreamy chocolate cake in the form of God's words? I promise you won't gain a pound, but you might lose tons of worry and sorrow.

Dear God, thank you for your words of love, affirmation, and comfort for me. Please help me remember to reconnect with you daily, anchoring myself to your love and soothing my hurt feelings with the wonderful truth of your words.

The South Beached Whale Diet

by Michelle Rayburn

————◦—●◦●—◦————

*Blessed are those who hunger and thirst for
righteousness, For they shall be filled.*

MATTHEW 5:6 (NKJV)

RUMMAGING PAST CANS of green beans, cake mixes,
and some leftover stale butter mints from my parents'
anniversary party, I found nothing in the pantry to fit my mood.
Perhaps the refrigerator held some satisfaction. Nope. On to the
freezer. Zip. Zilch. Nothing. I had no idea what I wanted, so I
started back at the pantry for round two.

Within thirty minutes of settling on a bowl of chips and
settling my fanny on the sofa, I was back to the pantry-refrigerator-
freezer trifecta in search of something sweet. *Chocolate peanut
butter ice cream. Why didn't I see that before?* My South Beached
Whale Diet—a new twist on the Couch Potato Plan—was off to
a great start.

With my body and mind on repeat, I looped until my
sweatpants had no more stretch, and my tummy cried for an
antacid by sending a bile memo into my throat. Can I get a
witness? Perhaps you've tried this diet too.

*I think I'm full, but why am I still hungry? Who buys the food
around here anyway?*

It isn't only with food that I've lived this cycle of counterfeit hunger. I've presumed happiness dwelled in the place of bulging bank accounts and itty-bitty bills. Is there such a place?

Perhaps a bigger house with more storage would satisfy. Another degree for my resume or a shiny laptop for my newly decorated office would appease my hunger, wouldn't it? A thrilling hobby, a career shift, a shopping spree, a vacation, or a pedicure, but I still wouldn't know what I wanted.

Stuff doesn't bring us happiness. Neither does wealth or relationships or accolades. When a succession of options leads to unfulfillment, we may be seeking to satisfy a spiritual hunger with empty calories. Snacks. Stale butter mints. We find real contentment in God, in feasting on what matters to him and hungering for biblical truth. It's in thirsting for more of his character qualities and sampling opportunities with eternal impact. Those come packaged differently—sometimes messier and less glitzy—than spiritual junk food.

God promises to fill us when we hunger and thirst for his righteousness—for the things that align with his heart. There's no aimless searching to find this. He offers it freely for our growling spiritual stomachs when we read his Word, and the more we seek godliness, the more we'll hunger for it.

How is your appetite today? Are you craving what fulfills? When you follow God's satisfying plan, you might be surprised at how little you care for pursuits that have no eternal value.

Lord, help me not spoil my appetite on spiritual junk food instead of filling up on your soul-satisfying Word and will. Help me hunger for your qualities and thirst for your righteousness.

It's a Wonderful Body, Really

by Stephenie Hovland

*I praise you, for I am fearfully and
wonderfully made. Wonderful are your
works; my soul knows it very well.*

PSALM 139:14 (ESV)

IT WAS A dark and sweaty night . . .

Once again, I was wide awake at 3:00 a.m. Once again, I was drenched in night sweats and threatening to spontaneously combust. Once again, I was steaming mad.

And then, questions started to fill my mind:

- Do I need to drink more water during the day because of my midnight bathroom runs and hot flashes?

- Does this count as exercise? I'm certainly sweating enough for a good half-hour aerobics class.

- Does my husband ever roll over and think I've wet the bed?

- Have I ever wet the bed and just thought it was night sweats?

Sometimes I remain irritable for the rest of the night, upset that my perimenopausal body keeps disrupting good sleep. Then, I argue that the sleep wasn't really that good anyway, so maybe it's a welcome interruption. I can never get comfortable for more than ten seconds.

Eventually, I pray and ask God a few things:

- Are you amused when I go to bed cold with wool socks and flannel only to frantically strip an hour later?

- Do you chuckle when I can't sleep half the night nor stay awake most of the day?

- Is "fearfully and wonderfully made" really the best description for this mess of a body?

And then I pray blessings over my body—this flesh that is a gift from God, an often-aggravating puzzle God has given to me to figure out. Body part by body part, I ask God to bless each one. I start at my toes and work my way to my nose. I notice that as I pray for my bunions and calloused feet, I start to get less agitated. The varicose veins, poochy stomach, and flabby arms all get their due. I relax and dedicate each aging part to God's work and service to my neighbor. I pray they will help me be the light that shines for other people, no matter how flawed I am. By the time I get to blessing my foggy brain, I have either fallen back to sleep or forgotten what I was doing in the first place.

While we live on this earth, we will have to live with bodies that remind us of both the blessings and disappointments. Let's find some humor in our disappointments and support one another in all stages of life.

Creator, I often don't fully appreciate the body you have given me. Please let me see how it has been wonderfully made. Help me use my body to serve you and serve others.

Our
Contributors

KRISTINE ACCOLA has faced insur-mountable odds and overcame them by God's mercy and grace. He redirected her path. Kris believes joy is in the journey, and the adventure is where God has you. She writes fiction that points toward God for the solution to any problem. She surrounds herself with family and friends at home, and at her day job she serves as a church administrative assistant. She can be reached at misskay.accola@gmail.com.

EVA BURKHOLDER (MACE, Columbia International University) is a missionary kid, wife, mother of two sons and a daughter-in-law, former cross-cultural worker, and a missionary member care provider. She invites women to slow down, listen, and reflect on God's Word through her blog (www.evaburkholder.com) and her book, *Favored Blessed Pierced: A Fresh Look at Mary of Nazareth.* Eva rejuvenates by doing macramé and baking.

MINDY CANTRELL is a women's min-istry leader and devotional writer who passionately shares a little hope and a lot of grace with every soul she meets. Mindy has enjoyed following her husband of 27 years across the United States and to the Marshall Islands, creating and leading in women's ministries wherever they landed. Come find some hope and grace where Mindy blogs at www.mindycantrell.com.

MARY CURCIO is a retired teacher and school administrator. Currently, she is the women's ministry leader at her home church. Her passion is teaching and writing about God's Word. She has taught women's Bible studies and Sunday school for over 30 years. In her new writing endeavors, she writes devotionals and is working on her first book. She can be found as @mary.o.curcio on Facebook.

EDNA EARNEY, a retired senior English teacher, has graduated from her colleagues' go-to proofreader to freelance writer. She is happiest when communicating about transformations—moments that make life's pressured times worth the work. She has written for and edited two books. When the day's work is done, look for Edna swinging on her back porch in Southeast Texas, sipping a glass of sweet tea with her husband. Contact Edna at mrsearney@gmail.com.

 **SALLY FERGUSON'S** devotionals have been published in *Pathways to God* and *Light From The Word*. She's also written for *Just Between Us, Thriving Family, Upgrade with Dawn, Almost an Author,* and *ezinearticles.com*. Her e-book, *How to Plan a Women's Retreat* is available on Amazon. Sally's next project is a Bible study for caregivers. She lives in the beautiful countryside of Jamestown, New York, with her husband and her dad. Visit Sally's blog at www.sallyferguson.net.

 **NANCY GRAVES** is a freelance writer and editor. She is the author of print and online articles, a blog contributor, and a member of several book launch teams. As an adult student, she served on the staff of her college newspaper, *The Tartan*, for many years, eventually stepping into the role of editor in chief. She is the recipient of several ICCJA awards. She writes fiction and nonfiction in various genres. Nancy can be reached at nleegraves@gmail.com.

 **DARLA GRIECO**, a wife and mother of four, is passionate about her love for Jesus and for the written word. Darla combines the knowledge she gained from her MSEd in psychology with all she has learned on her spiritual journey to encourage other women to grow in their faith and identity. She shares lessons she's learned about reading, writing, and redemption at www.dsgrieco.com.

MARY HARKER started a passage to writing following a nursing career. She is passionate about inspiring women to walk with Jesus in truth, freedom, and hope and leads a women's Bible study at her church. She lives near Rockford, Illinois, with her husband, James, and son, Drew. When not writing, Mary can be found walking and meeting new people in her neighborhood or reading one of her favorite authors. Connect with her at harker.mary96@gmail.com.

A pastor's wife, former teacher, and mother of two grown girls, **STEPHENIE HOVLAND** helps others connect to God. She finds unique ways each of us can kindle the fires of our faith-filled lives. She's the first to admit she has plenty to work on. Join Stephenie as she walks alongside other Christian women, sharing weaknesses and strengths, supporting one another. You can find Stephenie's devotion booklets at CreativeCommunications.com and her contact information at www.stepheniehovland.com.

BECKI JAMES is an ally to all who desire to live in God's presence. With an "old friend" flair, she is a voice of reason, gently guiding hearts to God's throne. Whether ministering with pen or microphone, Becki's way with words nurture Christ's love to all ages. Becki is a registered nurse who lives with her husband and family in New York. She enjoys decorating, resting beside the water, and hosting a table of friends.

LORI LIPSKY writes short fiction and poetry. Her character-driven stories point readers to a fresh perspective. Friends, family relationships, and the arts are common themes in her work. Her writing has appeared in *The Avalon Literary Review, Penwood Review, Mature Living Magazine, Every Day Poems, Spelk, Poppy Road Review,* and various other publications. Lori's collection of flash fiction stories, *Only One Rachmaninoff,* is due to release in 2021. Learn more at www.lorilipsky.com.

SANDY LIPSKY is new to writing. She worked as a nurse and music teacher before exploring this current endeavor. Her first publication appeared in *Focus on the Family Magazine.* She believes her faith, family, and friends are most important. After errands, cooking, gardening, and cleaning, you can find her writing with her faithful dog snoring nearby. Sandy lives in Georgia with her husband, daughter, and loyal canine.

CHARLAINE MARTIN is a writer, speaker, certified personal trainer, and blogger. She lives with her Second Blessing, her second husband, in the Thumb of Michigan. They share a love of flying, cycling, and traveling to enjoy time with their children and grandchildren. Her blog covers health, remarriage, Christian faith, and other God-adventure topics on her website www.charlainemartin.com. She also leads Healthy Lifestyles groups with her ministry Be Totally Fit for Life!

DIANA LEAGH MATTHEWS has numerous stories to share, often from her job as an activities director, where she wears many hats including Bible teacher, vocalist, historian, and event planner. She has four prayer books scheduled for publication in 2021. Check out her hymn stories and Bible studies at www.dianaleaghmatthews.com and her *hymn-votions* on social media.

TLC NIELSEN loves books so much she gets paid to be around them in a school library. Her first ever novel, *By Land or Sea*, is in the editing stage, which makes her appreciate every book she's ever read. In her free time, TLC enjoys being the assistant editor for the Word Weavers newsletter, book judge for various author contests, and a jazz trombonist in two area big bands. Find her on Bookstagram and Goodreads.

MICHELLE RAYBURN wants to help you discover the joy of finding God in the most unexpected places. She's an award-winning author and podcaster who emphasizes how life's difficulties can turn out to be opportunities to learn and grow. Michelle has an MA in ministry leadership with a pastoral counseling emphasis. She's been married to her husband, Phil, for more than 31 years, and they've successfully launched two sons into adulthood. www.michellerayburn.com

JOANIE SHAWHAN is a Selah Awards finalist for *In Her Shoes: Dancing in the Shadow of Cancer.* She is an ovarian cancer survivor, registered nurse, speaker, and media guest. She speaks to medical students in the Survivors Teaching Students program and co-founded an ovarian cancer social group, The Fried Eggs—Sunny-Side Up. When not attending her book clubs or writing critique group, Joanie enjoys swimming, knitting, and learning to play the autoharp.

ROBIN STEINWEG finds life is "Sweet in the Middle"—like the creamy center of a sandwich cookie! Her writing can be found at *The Christian Pulse, Keys for Kids, Just 18 Summers, The Upper Room, The Secret Place, Today's Christian Woman,* and *Music Teacher's Helper* blog. Read her daily prayers for parents on @Prayerenting on Facebook and bits of positivity with songs on her YouTube channel, both found at www.robinsteinweg.com.

After years of living in fear and defeat, **GINA STINSON** is busy reclaiming every day for God's glory. She is a pastor's wife and mom of two teenagers. Her recent book, *Reclaimed: The Stories of Rescued Moments and Days*, is a storytelling devotional for those who are searching for hope and humor for everyday living. You can learn more about Gina at www.ginastinson.com or on her Facebook page, where she shares weekly devotions and encouragement.

KATHY CARLTON WILLIS is "God's Grin Gal." She writes and speaks with a balance of funny and faith—whimsy and wisdom. Over a thousand of Kathy's articles have been published, and she has several books in her Grin Gal brand. Kathy graduated with honors from Bible college and has served 30+ years in full-time ministry. Check out her Grin & Grow Break video devotions on social media.

LISA-ANNE WOOLDRIDGE is an author and speaker who resides in the San Francisco Bay Area with her husband and three children. She is a serial contributor to anthologies, a former newspaper columnist, and is perpetually at work on a new novel. After decades of ministry, Lisa-Anne has turned to writing full time and hopes to help others "Live Life Illuminated." Find out more about Lisa-Anne at www.lisa-anne.net.

Acknowledgments

This book was made possible due to some very special people. We want to acknowledge their support and help.

We have grateful gratitudes for:

Our buddy editors. Each devotion was edited by at least one buddy editor before the contributing author submitted the piece. Some devotions had input from multiple buddies. We couldn't have done this project without you. In addition to the contributing authors helping each other (a beautiful thing to watch!), we had the benefit of feedback from: Anita Klumpers, Sue Smith, Beth Barron, Rachel Kerstetter, Jessica Birdwell, and Shannon Landon. Thank you for your attention to detail and your willingness to edit free of charge.

Our editors. Kathy Carlton Willis and Michelle Rayburn edited the complete book. Thank you for polishing our content and making our words shine.

Our families and friends. They cheered us on and managed without us so we could write. They support our dreams and make us feel like we're rock stars. This book is possible in part because of you.

Our book designer, Michelle Rayburn. You made sure the book cover design and the interior design reflected our WordGirls brand as well as our hearts. We are so proud of our beautiful book because of your creative talent.

Our churches. We value the fellowship of faith. Because of our heavenly Father, we are family.

Our Lord. May this book bring you all the glory. It is because of you and your Word that we have words. We are pleased to be your WordGirls.

Made in the USA
Columbia, SC
20 March 2021